BRIAN SAMPSON

EXPLORING AND
EXPLOITING
NEW MARKETS
FOR
PROFITABLE BUSINESS GROWTH

EXPLORING AND EXPLOITING NEW MARKETS
FOR
PROFITABLE BUSINESS GROWTH

ALAN W. BARRELL

Published in association with the Institute of Directors

DIRECTOR BOOKS

Published by Director Books,
an imprint of Fitzwilliam Publishing Limited,
Simon & Schuster International Group,
Fitzwilliam House, 32 Trumpington Street,
Cambridge CB2 1QY, England

First published 1990

© Alan W. Barrell

British Library Cataloguing in Publication Data

Barrell, Alan W.
Exploring and exploiting new markets.
1. Marketing
I. Title
658.8

ISBN 1-870555-20-1

Designed by Geoff Green
Typeset by Quorn Selective Repro Ltd
Printed in Great Britain by BPCC Wheatons Ltd, Exeter

CONTENTS

CONTENTS

PREFACE

Profitable growth is the life-blood of any thriving business. This holds whether an enterprise is working in manufacturing and marketing or in the service sector, whether it is operating in industrial business fields or selling perishable consumer goods. Commodity businesses, high-technology businesses, consulting services, financial services, any organisation seeking profitable business growth is essentially looking for markets to exploit. It follows that in an increasingly competitive world and at a time when business methods are becoming more and more sophisticated, with the continued development of information technology providing the means for ever faster decisions and action, chairmen, directors and other senior executives are often faced with a bewildering spectrum of choices when deciding how to keep their companies growing at appropriate rates and in circumstances of finite resources.

The idea for this book came from discussions of this kind of problem and its aims are simply:

- To capture the attention of company chairmen, chief executives and other directors and direct their thinking towards the potential for profitable growth in finding and exploiting new markets.
- To provide *practical* advice, guidance and to share experiences with readers to enable strategy, direction and plans to emerge in companies and for these to be implemented quickly – and thus to enable early successes and measurable business results.
- To identify the role of top management in *leading* the initiatives necessary to get companies moving faster than competitors in market development, particularly related to competition.

British companies will be particularly interested in competitive positioning relative to US and Japanese industry and the emergence of the single European market which will affect millions of us from 1992. *All* companies with international pretensions, including those based in Japan and the USA, will likewise want to be fully informed about the new pattern of global business dynamics which the single market in Europe will bring about.

Any book of this kind is the product of personal experiences and preferences and biases will show through from time to time. The focus throughout is on relating things which have happened or been observed to coincide with theory and on the kinds of experiences companies are likely to have, simply because in business it really is 'results that count' and results come only from successful business practice. Many of the situation reports and examples I have used are based upon significant periods in marketing and general management in two outstanding companies: Baxter Healthcare, and the Domino Group.

I have learned a great deal over the years from a great many people in management and in other positions in a number of companies. I acknowledge all of the help that I have received and the good advice and teaching. This is not in any sense a catalogue of my original thought but a summary of knowledge and perhaps a little wisdom of which I have essentially been the beneficiary during my extremely interesting life in business.

CHAPTER 1

————————— ·❧· —————————

FIRST PRINCIPLES

- Customers are the most important decision-makers (not managers) in determining the success of a business.
- To satisfy customers consistently the first thing a company needs is to have very clear aims and objectives. These must be shared collectively throughout the company.

WHAT IS A CUSTOMER?

If you believe this is a strange question, reflect for a moment on your own business and ask yourself who *your* customers are. If you are a provider of consulting services this will be a simple question: you will have clients. If, however, your company makes pharmaceutical products which are distributed world-wide through a complicated distribution chain and if your company has subsidiary companies in different parts of the world, you may find that your central organisation has customers who are subsidiary companies and customers who are wholesale distributors; further down the line there will be customers who are retail distributors and, indeed, customers who do not handle your product directly at all – the doctors who prescribe; finally, the consumer and the end-user customer is the patient who is receiving the therapy. We see different kinds of distribution chain in industrial marketing. Customers can include distributors, agents, manufacturers' representatives and other kinds of middle men, and at the end of the chain for any industrial or consumer product there is the end-user.

All of this may sound extremely fundamental. And so it is. But it is astonishing how often companies still attempt to develop products from ideas generated within the firm, and embark with enthusiasm on expensive marketing exercises with products and services which are in no way in tune with the feelings, needs and motivations of customers and which may be presented in such a way that they are incompatible with the aims, ambitions

and motivations of distributors and other middle men essential to the success
of marketing the product.

Only on an individual basis can companies decide who their customers
are. It should be one of the first critical questions asked when companies
are starting up or when a strategic review is being undertaken in an existing
or maturing organisation.

CUSTOMER DECISION CRITERIA

Company directors should reflect regularly on the way in which customers,
once identified and categorised, make their decisions. Customer decision
criteria are, of course, of extreme importance and by careful market
research, knowledge and experience of a business built up over a number
of years, and through plain common sense, we may find out in any sort of
business those things which will cause the customer to make a decision in
one direction or another. I suggest that it is extremely important to prevent
the analysis of customer decision criteria becoming purely mechanical and
statistical. Factual information and statistics are unquestionably important.
However, the human dimension in customer decision-making is a critical
one and senior management is wise to think about it. Customers of consumer
products, industrial products, or services are obviously interested in quality
and value. How we define quality and value is a crucial issue, and again
we must consider these criteria from the customer's standpoint rather than
our own.

In industrial marketing, where manufacturing companies are buying capital
equipment, the reliability of the machinery which they purchase is of extreme
importance since it will be required to keep their production lines running.
In industrial fields the 'completeness' of products can be a crucial factor
for customers; decisions to purchase from one supplier or another may very
well not be based on purely economic grounds but on an understanding
that a particular company has a reputation for providing completeness in
what it offers. This might mean equipment, computer software, installation,
training of staff, outstanding after-sales service and technical information.
This principle also holds true in many service industries where clients do
not simply wish to pay for a report but want a more complete product from a
consulting firm and may wish the firm to proceed beyond the point of analysis
to implement the proposed programme. The situation in a consumer business
such as food and beverages may be somewhat different, although even here
customer services and benefits beyond the product itself are often offered
as an inducement to exploit a market or gain a larger market share – for
example, free cinema tickets have been offered with wine boxes. In fields

such as pharmaceuticals and medical products, the decision-making part of the customer chain, which is often the position of surgeon or nursing officer, may be largely influenced by the knowledge that a particular company does offer 'complete products' – in other words, a system of drug therapy or a piece of equipment backed up by scientific information, technical service, seminars and appropriate medical information.

The critical point here is that in directing a business for long-term growth and stability, the chairman, directors and senior management should take sufficient time to consider the particular supplier–buyer relationship which is most likely to bring success in their particular field. Trust, confidence, rapport between people and a feeling on the part of the customer that the supplying company is truly seeking an understanding of his or her needs and problems, are still issues of crucial importance in terms of competitive business activity. Price is an important part of any buying decision process, but value for the investment made is the real consideration which will be top of the list of most customers.

COMPANY-WIDE QUALITY PROGRAMMES

The more traditional interpretation of the word 'quality' in the business setting – and especially in manufacturing industry – has come to mean quality control, with an emphasis on statistical analysis. Using this approach, products are checked at various points in the production process or a statistical sample is taken for checking and batches of product are either accepted or rejected. Thankfully, this narrow approach is being superseded by a much more expansive and exciting approach with great potential for business. A company-wide approach to a philosophy and practice of total quality and an aim towards zero defects can, if properly instituted, bring about vast improvements in attitude, can result in the establishment of ambitious and clear objectives, and can bring a tremendous sense of purpose to a whole organisation. Examples of the changes which can be wrought by a structured approach to company-wide quality and practice are provided by the progress made during 1985–7 by the Jaguar car company and, during roughly the same period, by British Airways (BA). In both cases, there has been an enormous change in the company's image in customers' eyes over a short span of time. Both were in some senses regarded as a joke. Both are now regarded as leaders in their field.

Jaguar, led by John Egan, invested millions of pounds in the almost complete redesign of its executive cars and the complete retraining of its entire workforce to understand and meet the needs, in terms of both functionality and quality of service, of discerning customers world-wide. Competing with BMW and

Mercedes in particular, the newly privatised Jaguar, broken loose from years of mediocrity within the giant nationalised British Leyland Group, changed identity and direction within a one-and-a-half-year time-span. The result was a move into profitability through world-wide growth, with particular progress in the lucrative US prestige car market.

If anything the changes at BA have been more dramatic, and many of us have seen and felt these changes taking place as we have travelled around the world on different airlines. The Scandinavian airline, SAS, has followed the BA example, and a very long list of companies which have also made the investment in a structured approach to company-wide quality could be assembled: Rank Xerox, IBM, and Phillips are but three.

In a properly organised company-wide quality programme, the concept of the *primacy of the customer* is central. However, the concept of 'customer' is no longer understood simply as the agency or client receiving the goods or services of the enterprise. Since teamwork and the unity of all company members behind the principle of product quality are essential to success in a competitive world, different individuals and groups within the company are encouraged to think of themselves as both suppliers and customers. If the purchasing manager, for instance, fails to obtain the components required by the production supervisor on time, then he is essentially letting an internal customer down and that internal customer, who may be a supplier of a sub-assembly to another department, is also at risk of letting another internal customer down. Enormous gains can be enjoyed if individuals and groups in companies can be encouraged to think of each other as customers and suppliers and can be stimulated to generate the kind of response that an aggressive customer generally seeks in a world where there are choices. Of course, everyone in the company is also encouraged and trained to think of the person or organisation in the great wide world outside who is the ultimate receiver of the goods or services being offered, but it remains the case that unless quality is built into products and services at every step of preparation, and teamwork and inter-departmental co-operation are outstanding, the customer on the outside will not be satisfied.

Company-wide quality programmes have the potential for enormous improvements in efficiency and in the reduction of costs. The 'cost of quality' is often spoken of these days and the meaning is really 'cost of poor quality or a standard less than zero defect'. Expressing the cost of quality can be an interesting exercise for a company or for departments within it and can form the basis of goal-setting prior to initiating improvements.

To set up, to structure and to lead a company-wide quality improvement programme takes specialist knowledge, energy and skill. In some companies where a quality assurance manager is in place, he or she would be the person to do the job. In smaller companies company-wide quality programmes can be organised by specialist agencies. There are plenty of consulting services and a growing number of books on the subject, some of which are listed in the bibliography. It is essential for success in building a company-wide quality programme that the chairman, directors and all senior executives are seen to be completely committed to the effort. Many companies begin by establishing a quality policy such as that shown in Example 1.1. One way forward is for a quality assurance manager, possibly with outside help, to run a quality awareness programme for board members. All employees in the company could subsequently participate in a similar awareness programme in groups of appropriate size, and in each case the chairman or chief executive could introduce and chair the meeting to show, by participating and sharing, the commitment of senior management to the effort. Suitable audio-visual material can be obtained for use as part of these programmes and many companies choose to bring their own identity to the material which is produced to accompany the workshop sessions. Material used by Domino Printing Sciences plc is reproduced here as an example of the way in which this can be attractively done.

Beyond the initial quality awareness activity there is obviously a requirement for directors and management constantly to reinforce the principles that have been established in the programme, and the quality assurance manager or the outside advisers will be required to do follow-up training. Some companies use the medium of the company newspaper or produce a special 'quality newsletter' to keep everyone informed on quality issues.

It must be stressed that the concept of total quality which is being discussed here is not a concept of technical correctness of a piece of equipment nor simply the meeting of a bland specification. Quality in the customer's mind relates simply to complete 'fitness for my purpose'. In industrial business fields this goes far beyond whether a piece of electronic equipment has been properly assembled and tested. Total quality embraces the issues of specification, planning, shipment and installation, meeting the delivery deadlines and the price quoted as well as the technical performance and in-field servicing after sale of the item.

Company-wide quality also extends to the way in which the customer is received on a visit or on the telephone. It embraces the way customers are treated on administrative matters. It is, first and foremost, a matter of *attitude*. Response to the customer's needs and requirements is the primary goal and the main focus of all employees in companies committed to quality improvement. The Japanese in the past decade and, in some aspects of industrial marketing, the Germans, have shown that customer loyalty can be unshakeable – not by quoting the lowest prices, but by developing a relationship of trust and confidence and providing, in line with the customer's precise needs, a continuity and quality of offering which surpasses anything the competition has been able to do. In Britain, the USA and in other parts of the developed world, the lessons are being learnt and company-wide quality programmes are being employed successfully in more and more companies.

The company-wide quality concept can be effectively reinforced after the initial awareness training by having members of the board and the senior management team 'sponsor' key customers. In this process, which is especially applicable to industrial manufacturing and marketing companies, the 'sponsor' undertakes to visit the customer at least once a year, to talk by telephone at least two or three times a year, and to be available for contact at other times should the customer require access. The benefits of this type of approach are twofold. The director or senior manager is given a continual insight into the realities of serving customers and is forced to think about the needs of customers, and at the same time the customer is made to feel especially important and well looked after.

The assumption is being made during this part of the book that those reading it are committed to the concept of directors and senior executives taking a lead and a direct interest in customer relations and adopting a philosophy of very strong and inspirational leadership to forge a strong quality culture and to remove barriers which can exist between layers of management, operating divisions, subsidiary companies, and so on. These thoughts lead naturally to consideration of the company's aims and objectives, and how these may be established, clarified and shared, how commitment to them may be won, and how they may be transformed into actions and then into sales and profit growth.

Example 1.1 Problem-solving Philosophy and Techniques

As part of a company-wide quality programme, an acceptance by employees throughout an organisation of responsibility for answering customer questions or solving problems, or at least for seeing to it that a problem-solving pathway is established, is very important.

Domino
COMPANY-WIDE
QUALITY IMPROVEMENT

Domino

OBJECTIVES OF CWQI

To bring about a Fundamental Change in the way we Manage our Business, and in doing so, Improve our Customer Image, Product Quality, the Cost Competitiveness of our Products, and the overall Efficiency of our Organisation.

COMPANY-WIDE QUALITY IMPROVEMENT

Domino

Our Quality Policy

We must ensure that our present and future customers are always satisfied with the products and services which we provide.

Every Domino customer must find that:

- **They can communicate with us.**

- **We listen and respond to their needs.**

- **We are reliable and do what we say we will do.**

- **We deliver the right products on time, every time.**

- **We are aiming for zero defects in all our products, services, information and advice.**

The aim of Domino's Zero Defect Quality Policy is not restricted to products alone, but also applies to those tasks carried out by all employees. Zero Defect Quality demands that each of us is right first time in every task we undertake. Total customer satisfaction will only be achieved when we conduct our internal daily operations as if we were each others customers.

Our collective task is to increase customer satisfaction throughout our whole organisation and into the external markets for our products and services.

Alan Barrell
Chief Executive
Domino Printing Sciences plc.
Cambridge, England.

1 March 1989

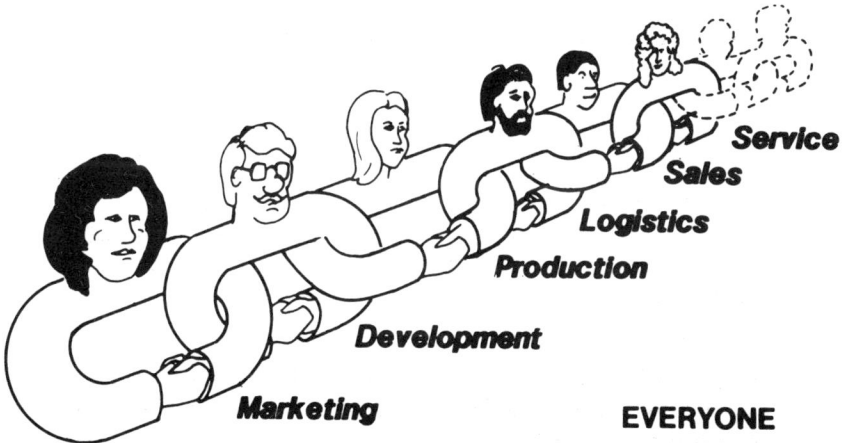

QUALITY IS

CUSTOMER SERVICE

Service
Sales
Logistics
Production
Development
Marketing

**EVERYONE
HAS HIS
CUSTOMER**

HELP STRENGTHEN THE CHAIN

THE COMPANY — AIMS AND OBJECTIVES

In American business in particular, one reads and hears these days a very great deal about the need to define the overall 'mission' of a company. What this word means should be obvious, but some boards and executives in Europe do not like the ring of it. The purpose here is not to argue about the merits of different words, the issue at stake is the need to identify clearly the overall sense of purpose of an enterprise. What are we here for? What are we doing? What are our aims? How can we in one or two sentences express the basis of our goals and desires as a group of people? To illustrate the kind of purpose or mission statement I have in mind, I have taken from annual reports the two extracts reproduced in Examples 1.2 and 1.3.

Despite the cynicism which one sometimes finds levelled at this kind of process, it is often the case that in companies where a very clear sense of purpose has been distilled, and where management has been able to get employees from all parts of the enterprise to participate in the establishment of the statement of purpose – and, furthermore, to believe in it implicitly – the commitment, the sense of purpose, the *esprit de corps* which can be generated, are of great potential in enabling purposeful action to take place.

There are two basic approaches to the development of a mission or purpose statement; these are illustrated, for a company of medium to large size, in Figure 1.1. The chairman and chief executive, with the assistance of the board, can sit in the boardroom and issue the 'company credo'. (Figure 1.1a). There are many examples of where this has been done successfully. The other approach is illustrated in Figure 1.1b. The board generates a number of ideas and invites feedback on them from employees at all levels. This feedback can be channelled through line managers, who can discuss it and distil it into a series of proposals which is made available to the board to learn from, debate and adjust, with a mission statement emerging as a result. This alternative approach is often far more effective. Even if the board decides that the final proposals are not entirely appropriate, it has the authority to make changes. Provided these do not completely turn the previous work on its head, and provided they are well explained, the value of the process of earlier participation and discussion will not generally be lost.

Whichever process is used, the eventual output can be attractively written up and presented to employees in the form of a booklet. Such material is not only extremely valuable in generating new impetus and momentum among existing employees, but can also be used effectively for recruitment and the orientation and induction of new recruits. Many companies in recent years have included this kind of information in annual reports and accounts, thereby also providing shareholders with very clear messages about identity

Example 1.2

Metal Box plc / Report and Accounts 1988

Metal Box is one of the world's leading manufacturers of food and beverage packaging, speciality packaging and engineering systems. It is also a leader in heating and bathroom products and cheques and business forms. It operates through subsidiaries, joint ventures and related companies in 23 countries. Using its technological strength, product quality and commitment to customer service it aims to build on those strengths and continuously improve its competitive position.

The focus of the Group strategy is:
- to concentrate efforts on strengthening and expanding core businesses;
- to maintain technological leadership and provide excellence in customer service, design and quality;
- to extend activities internationally, particularly in Europe, the Americas and Asia Pacific;

so as to achieve increasing real returns to shareholders in both earnings per share and dividends.

Example 1.3

The BOC Group has an international and world-competitive portfolio of businesses. Our principal businesses are industrial gases and health care products and services. The Group also has significant interests in distribution services and in high vacuum technology. We are a world leader in these businesses. We operate in more than fifty countries and employ some 40 000 people.

The BOC Group plc

(a)

Chairman
|
Board
|
The Company Credo
The Mission
|
Communicated
world-wide
↙↓↘
But a one-way
process

(b)

Board
|
Issues outline and ideas
↙↓↘
World-wide
|
Invites feedback
and
builds feedback structure

- Operating units
- Through managers
- Response and other
  thoughts/inputs

Final form of Mission
is announced and
published with
acknowledgement to everyone

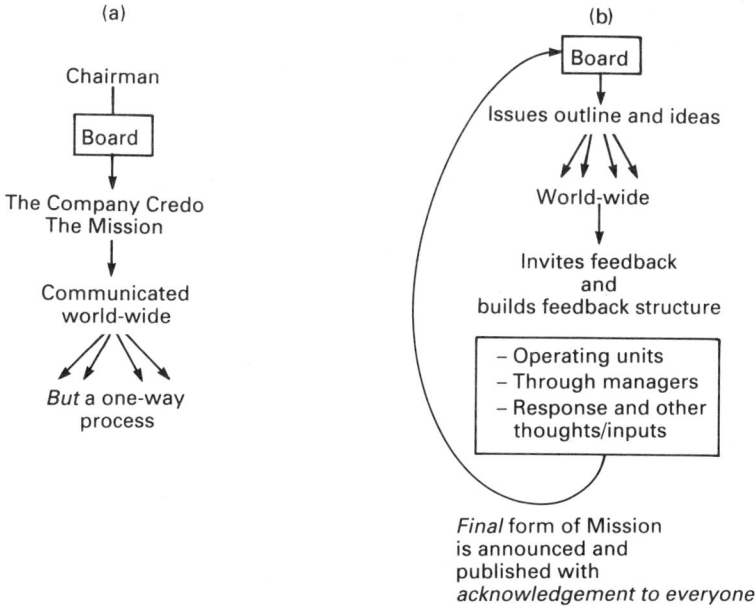

Figure 1.1 Two approaches to establishing company mission or purpose

and purpose. Institutional and private investors are extremely interested in this kind of information, which helps to strengthen the bonds between companies, directors and those who own the company. The kind of output which can be achieved and expressed in a very simple form, which is then available for everyone in the company to work by, is reproduced in Example 1.4.

The importance of the roles of chairman and directors in leading and supporting the process whereby the aims and objectives of companies are distilled, revisited, expressed, re-expressed, communicated and subsequently reinforced and worked to, cannot be overemphasised. Even in small companies with a handful of people, common purpose and identity with a cause is a great motivator. Human beings and the collective wisdom of groups large and small are tremendously powerful weapons which chairmen, directors and boards can control if sufficient time and attention are paid to creating in the company an appropriate environment and to enabling sufficient participation in defining purpose and goals.

In this chapter we have spent substantial time focusing on customers. It cannot be denied that customers *are* the most important decision-makers in determining the success of a business. Exploring and exploiting new markets means satisfying more customers in new fields. So the principle is of primary importance; to be equipped to explore and exploit new markets and to take maximum benefit from this exercise, a company needs to have very clear aims and objectives which are shared throughout the enterprise. The building of these kinds of foundations is a prerequisite in today's competitive world to doing battle with the international competition that is likely to be found in any new market of substantial value.

Example 1.4

Domino   Domino Printing Sciences plc

Aims and Objectives

These aims and objectives of the Company have been developed by Domino's Management Team and represent a consensus of feeling about our company.

Our aims as a group of companies

We, the Domino team, intend to become world leaders in electronic overprinting by:

- Developing technology that meets the needs of our customers
- Delivering quality products on time
- Giving support our customers can rely on
- Efficiently managing our business through planning and control without bureaucracy
- Promoting employee pride and satisfaction through participation and reward
- Generating an attractive rate of return for our investors

Domino related success factors

To achieve our aim requires a successful team that:

- Has common goals with clear objectives
- Thinks internationally
- Encourages innovation
- Communicates clearly
- Plans its resources and meets commitments
- Operates simple procedures
- Accepts responsibility
- Respects the individual

◆ **Domino**   Domino Printing Sciences plc

Customer related success factors

Our success depends upon Domino achieving greater customer satisfaction than our competitors in all these related areas:

SUPPORT
- Fast response
- Listen to feedback
- Knowledgeable staff
- Customer training

PRODUCTS
- Fit for purpose
- Good quality
- Value for money

IMAGE
- Good reputation
- Honesty & integrity
- Personal contact

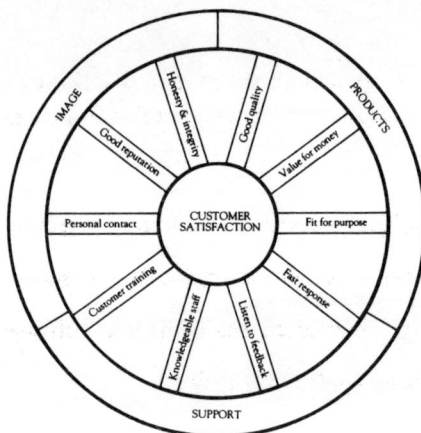

We all have a part to play in supporting the hub of our business – CUSTOMER SATISFACTION.

Our place within industry and the community

We intend to remain a socially responsible company within the community and a good employer by:

- Being an attractive and exciting organisation to work with
- Providing good prospects and remuneration
- Promoting good working conditions, social activities and a friendly atmosphere
- Increasing local prosperity
- Encouraging links between education and industry

- Respecting the environment
- Supporting local charities and community activities
- Maintaining an honest and professional image

CHAPTER 2

∽

IDENTIFYING AND CATEGORISING MARKETS

'Markets' are spoken about as if they fall into a simple descriptive pattern. What kinds of market can you think of? You may come up with an answer something like this:

- Geographical – continent, country, region.

- Consumer – numerous segments and sub-segments.

- Industry – numerous segments and sub-segments.

- Product or application-related.

This is clearly an oversimplification, although it is a start in unravelling the complexity of identifying markets.

Unless we describe the 'market' we are attempting to explore and exploit, our efforts cannot begin with any degree of assurance of success. Clarity of focus and purpose in describing markets, understanding them and exploring them, is of paramount importance especially when considering entering markets new to the company, since major investments may be required to mount a campaign with a new product in a new market, much or all of which can be completely wasted if the product–market match is incorrect. Even at the simplest level, any new marketing venture should be undertaken with careful forethought and preparation. For example, a company which has been extremely successful in providing a product or service to customers in the UK but has no export experience would be well advised to adopt a carefully structured approach to decisions and action if the suggestion is made that France or Germany should be entered as the next stage in the growth of the organisation. Taking a product or service to one or more export markets is a very different proposition from entering a new region or customer applications segment in the home territory.

BUILDING A MARKET IDENTITY MATRIX

It is useful when considering the nature of markets to build upon the simple model featured at the beginning of the chapter and develop a matrix as shown in Figure 2.1 This enables a proposed new initiative to be examined relative to markets in stages. Geography is a good starting point for building the market matrix; and most companies will be very clear as to whether their focus is to be on consumer, industrial or other specialised markets. Having got this far, the consumer segments or industry segments can be drawn from established data. The Standard International Classification (SIC) system of markets is a very useful way of pinning down industry sectors with common terminology so that from country to country a marketing or a product manager will know that he or she is actually speaking about a market with consistent characteristics. Reproduced in Figure 2.2, from published data, is an extract to show the extent of classification of industrial activity by means of SIC codes.

How does this help us to explore and exploit new markets? On an international or individual country basis we can target our market research and our enquiries, our search for distributors and agents, our advertising and mailing, our exhibitions and promotions, within a framework known and acknowledged world-wide. Take, for example, SIC code 37202 Manufacture of Dental Instruments and Appliances. If we are an engineering company thinking of launching a new, small high-speed drill mechanism, before we take final decisions we can explore industry growth rates and trends in SIC category 37202; focus research more clearly on expected trends in the industry; and examine the specialist procedures and marketers who make up SIC 37202. If we are an international company we can have confidence that our groups in the USA and the Netherlands, for instance, can mount an equally thorough fact-based search of this industry sector, finding all appropriate manufacturers of dental instruments and appliances and gaining data on the size, scope and characteristics of a well-defined industry sector.

The SIC code system of identifying industry segments is not perfect – some companies are hard to pin down to a clear section. However, the system forces those, who market to industry, to *focus* and *define* segments and opportunity areas. It enables them to quantify by territory and/or major industrial activity *what* production people and packaging engineers are thinking, planning and doing. It enables them to be more precise in defining, for example, the number of filling lines extant for dairy equipment and the rate of likely growth of such lines. We can gain a clearer view of how many new pharmaceutical blister packing lines are planned for installation in the 1990s more efficiently, and quickly by using SIC data to target our

Geographical area	Type of industry	Specific application	Particular needs
UK France Germany Spain Italy Scandinavia Middle East Japan Australasia USA Canada Eastern Europe	Brewing Beverages Pharmaceutical Cosmetics Toiletries Food Automotive Wire and cable Printing Addressing General industry	Coding Dating Numbering Identification Bar codes Batching Logos Pricing Quality marking	Language Bar codes Computer networking Software Moving print heads Environmental issues Economy Multiple requirements Engineering support

Figure 2.1 Market identity matrix for product identification systems

35100	Manufacture of motor vehicles and their engines
35101	Manufacture of passenger cars
35102	Manufacture of commercial vehicles
35103	Manufacture of motor vehicle engines
35210	Manufacture of motor vehicle bodies
35220	Manufacture of trailers and semi-trailers
35230	Manufacture of caravans
35300	Manufacture of motor vehicle parts
36100	Shipbuilding and repairing
36101	Building or repairing inland water vessels
36102	Building or repairing pleasure boats and yachts
36103	Shipbreaking
36201	Manufacture of locomotives and parts
36202	Manufacture of other railway and tramway rolling stock and parts
36203	Repair of railway and tramway rolling stock
36300	Manufacture of cycles and motor cycles
36330	Manufacture of motorcycles and parts
36340	Manufacture of pedal cycles and parts
36400	Aerospace equipment manufacturing and repairing
36501	Manufacture of baby carriages
36502	Manufacture of other vehicles
37100	Manufacture of measuring, checking and precision instruments and apparatus
37201	Manufacture of medical, surgical and veterinary equipment
37202	Manufacture of dental instruments and appliances
37203	Manufacture of orthopaedic appliances and artificial limbs etc.
37310	Manufacture of spectacles and unmounted lenses
37320	Manufacture of optical precision instruments
37330	Manufacture of photographic and cinematographic equipment
37400	Manufacture of clocks, watches and other timing devices

Figure 2.2 Extract showing standard international classification system of markets

research candidates more precisely. We can also use rifle-shot rather than blunderbuss or shotgun techniques to assess the percentage penetration of our own product in defined market sectors or niches. In short, intelligent use of SIC classification data, available in all good reference libraries, can provide enhanced industry, market and competitor information, all on an international basis.

If we are looking only at geographical and demographic information, a wealth of data is available from a variety of sources – from government statistics to large numbers of both free and commercially offered publications. The studies made available by financial services firms such as Price Waterhouse of the economy, economic growth, population, demographics, industry base, currency, financial factors, etc., of the major countries of the world are invaluable and extremely readable for the director who wishes to get a quick idea of important economic and industrial factors for a specified area. *The Economist* also publishes data in various forms and regularly issues a hardback reference book, *The World in Figures,* which is an extremely useful reference guide for the director's shelf. The Department of Trade and Industry (DTI) is now the government department which embraces what was for years known as the British Overseas Trade Board. Summary and detailed information is available in its publications and from its library. Numerous firms offer specific reports on specified geographical areas, and the number of seminars and ancillary events available for briefing directors and managers is so great as to be confusing.

The most reliable approach to understanding markets, in a geographical category of course, is to employ people either directly or indirectly who are living and working on site or have done so extensively in the past. This is especially true for British and American companies which are attempting to penetrate Asian or Latin American markets. Language is a crucial factor, but no more so than a knowledge of culture and 'the way business is really done' (see Chapter 9). It can be extremely useful when considering approaching new markets to use a small focused independent consulting firm of two or three people who have lived and worked extensively in the territories and know how government, administration, industry, export and import, and all manner of other things are operated. It is foolhardy to believe that even in the largest companies we can always do all that is needed ourselves and have on hand all of the necessary expertise to operate fast-growing international business.

The example given below is an extract from a market research report on the UK electronic component market. It shows how data can be found and summarised to show how a particular market may be assessed in terms of numbers of lines or assembly stations.

Estimate of UK market size – Electronic component production

As stated earlier in this section, it is not valid to study this sector in terms of the value of turnover. Reported current employment figures are therefore used instead.

The various branches of the companies interviewed who gave line numbers, employed 5,500 people between them, and reported a total of 40 lines or assembly stations. The industry employs 91,000 people in total. On the basis of a simple extrapolation it is calculated that there are about 680 'lines' in the industry. However, since 400 of the companies in the electronics sector are very small manufacturers of printed circuit boards etc. and since the largest manufacturer of PCB reported that he was screen printing on one continuous line, this figure of 680 lines almost certainly is an overestimate.

PCBs represent 13% of the reported total worth of the electronics component industry, and 15% of employment. It is therefore considered that the estimate of lines should be put at a figure of about 600.

I have included the market category 'product- or application-related' in addition to the other possibilities described in the text and in the model, because in some areas of industrial marketing particular applications transcend the barriers between market segments. The need for computer control equipment and software to manage automated production lines, for instance, is not likely to be limited to any one manufacturing process or industry and the requirements of a number of different industry sectors may have many common threads for this kind of equipment, but only a small number of highly developed companies in each sector may be candidates for such equipment and such product application. Therefore, identifying 'the market' may require intensive study of target companies before any approaches are made to obviate the extensive waste of time and energy which could occur if all industry sectors are approached when, say, only 2 per cent are likely to have a requirement for such a product within a short time-span.

MEASURING MARKET OPPORTUNITY

Once a company board or a management group has established clear views and obtained good data about the existence of a market to exploit which could be entirely new or simply new to that company or its products (be they existing or new) it makes sense to begin to measure the opportunities which exist before reaching decisions on which markets to enter with particular products. It is possible to discover through published statistical information how many ice-cream filling and packing lines operate in many developed countries, how many breweries there are in Japan, and what the rate of output was during the last year of complete statistics. It is also possible to look ahead and forecast the number of new production lines which are likely to be installed in a particular industry in different countries, for example pharmaceutical products, and beyond this it is possible to predict how many of those pharmaceutical production lines during a particular period are likely to be devoted to liquid products and how many to solid dosage forms in blister packs. We can look ahead from a historical base of published data and predict how many new newspaper printing presses are likely to be installed during a period of time, and we can get a very good idea of the rate of replacement of this kind of equipment and many other industrial items. If the company is relatively small and has only one product it will still wish to optimise profitability by taking its product and its resources to those markets likely to provide the most attractive rates of return. It is useful to consider:

- Market information and where to find it.
- Market and marketing research.
- Assessing market maturity and growth potential.
- Competitive presence as a threat in 'new markets'.
- The director's role in decisions on market assessment, methodology and investment.

MARKET INFORMATION AND WHERE TO FIND IT

Very large companies are likely to have significant resources devoted to market research and market information. An in-house staff will maintain records of important markets, will access outside data to keep the information flowing, and will perform large and small research exercises with or without outside help. For the smaller company the situation can be bewildering. A highly experienced director of sales or marketing in certain industries may well have enormous knowledge of highly specialised markets which can be exploited without great expense on marketing research.

For most companies seeking to explore and exploit new markets, however, it is often necessary to gather data which are not available in-house. In the case of one company, scientists discovered a new test for cancer which had the potential of being developed into a laboratory test kit. This tiny start-up company faced the prospect of exploring UK and world market potential for a product which had not been offered before by any other organisation. And yet it found access to enormous quantities of published data on the incidence of different kinds of cancer; modes of treatment and success rates for different cancers; laboratory tests of somewhat similar type already available and the assessment of the usefulness of these; and the levels of investment in developed countries on cancer testing. It was possible for the small number of people running this company, who in some instances had in-depth knowledge of cancer therapy, to compile a comprehensive summary of the world-wide opportunity for the kind of product they envisaged developing, with very little expense and without the involvement of professional market research organisations. Part of their information-gathering exercise included the purchase of already published material, and it is worth remembering that in all significant market sectors industry associations are constantly publishing and updating market reference documents which can be purchased by anyone.

MARKET RESEARCH AND MARKETING RESEARCH

We need to distinguish between market research and marketing research. Understanding the facts about a market itself is one thing; having an understanding or making a forecast of the likely response to a marketing approach is something else. In many instances the basic data on market size and growth can be acquired. An outside market research firm can be assigned to this task and will help with data. For example, British Airways (BA) can quite easily discover how many passengers flew from London to a selection of North American cities every day and every week through 1988, and it can arrive at a composite number for the year. It can discover on which airline these customers flew, and it can easily project the likely number of passengers undertaking this kind of travel for 1990, 1991 and other years in the future. That is market research.

But BA executives may also want to know is how they can ensure that an increasing number of those transatlantic passengers sit on a BA aeroplane and consistently use BA as the airline of choice. Marketing research in this sense will mean investigating the motivations of travellers. Not many months ago when travelling to the USA, I was invited to spend some time in the first-class lounge testing with a skilled market research interviewer a wonderful new airline seat in which you could sit, sleep and probably do many other things. The questions were extremely carefully structured, down to the detail of accessibility of controls, position of head, and so on. I was also presented with the possibility of having a small personal video set with a selection of videos on the table-top in front of me and asked questions about this. There were numerous questions about whether and why I watched movies. BA spends many millions of pounds on this kind of research and the complex BA product, in addition to convenience of travel times, naturally includes the many considerations that a traveller has in mind when choosing a particular airline. The multi-million-pound investment in a small element of a complex product like transatlantic travel such as new seats or seat controls, needs to be carefully researched before the action is taken, to give a feeling of confidence in the outcome of the use of a significant amount of shareholders' funds.

ASSESSING MARKET MATURITY AND GROWTH POTENTIAL

The timing of entry into any kind of new market can be critical. Markets expand and markets contract. In Figures 2.3 and 2.4 the reader can see trends which have been recorded in specific industries or industry segments. In many cases the development of a new product takes a number of years, so that an understanding of the dynamics of market growth, market maturity and what is going on – in a competitive sense, a technology sense and environmentally, to name but three important aspects – is critical. There have been a number of examples described of companies of high repute entering markets at entirely the wrong time in the life cycle of the market or a product. If an entry is too early and fails an initiative may be written off, only for another company to appear perhaps two years later with an almost identical product and clean up because technology and/or environment in the industry in question have changed and made the offering more acceptable. Two good examples of this follow.

Example 2.1 Pharmaceutical Blister Packaging Equipment

The world has moved at differing rates to accept and employ new pharmaceutical products and new ways of packaging and securing medicines. A number of companies have produced equipment for encasing solid dosage forms of drugs in 'blister packages'. In some European countries there has been a rapid move to employ these newer techniques which bring the benefit of:

- Secure 'tamper-proof' encasement of tablets and capsules.
- Potential for 'original pack' dispensing, for example a thirty-day course of treatment in one or a number of blister cards. This obviates the need for pharmacies to open and count from larger

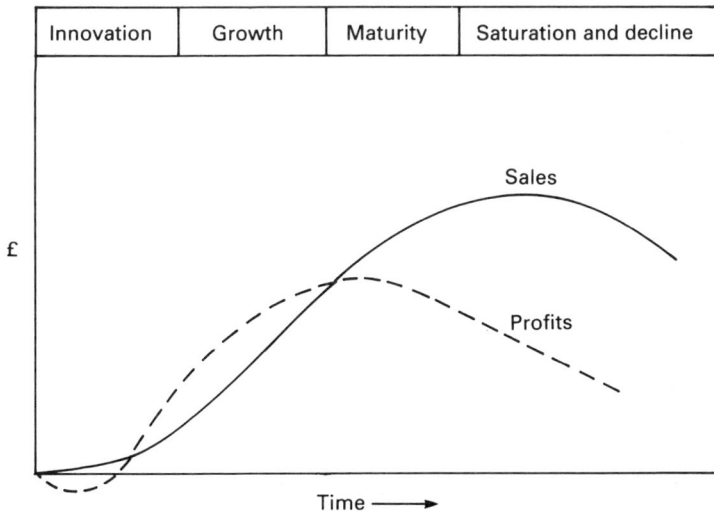

Figure 2.3 Product market growth and decline

packs, giving added efficiency within the supply chain and a continuity of 'tamper-proofness'.

- Potential to mark each blister (for example Monday, Tuesday, Wednesday, etc., or Day 1, Day 2, Day 3, etc.) to assist patient compliance in taking medication and the safer use of drugs.

Because of industry resistance or different rates of progress by bodies regulating medicines in different parts of the world, by the end of 1988, solid-dose drugs packed in blister packs in the USA (an 'advanced nation' on health issues!) had only reached 5 per cent of all solid-dose drugs sold, and in the UK had risen only to 25 per cent. In some other countries the percentage was, at the same time, between 50 per cent and 90 per cent.

Much time and promotional cost has been expended by some companies offering the equipment and plastic consumable materials for blister packages in the USA and UK to little avail, while other companies have focused on European countries where the industry trend towards acceptance and employment of the new packaging format has been particularly rapid.

Example 2.2 The Fruit Growing and Packing Industry in Chile

In the mid-to late 1970s, companies offering the kind of sophisticated equipment in use in Europe and California to assist the harvesting and packing of fruit felt that the time was not yet right for an attack on the Chilean fruit industry. The Chilean economy was in relatively poor shape and the industry was able to employ ample available low-cost labour – Chile had not become a major player on the world fruit export stage.

By 1988–89, after a number of years of running a market-led economy, with major incentives for exporters and a positive balance of trade, the Chilean fruit-growing and packing industry had become a significant supplier to Europe, the USA and Japan of fresh fruit and flash-frozen fruit such as kiwi fruit, melons (whole and 'melon balls'), oranges, peaches, apples, and soft fruits like strawberries and raspberries. Fruit packing has needed revolutionising to cope with the added volume and the need for processing (for example, freezing); with quality control – much demanded in the USA, Europe and Japan; with labelling; and with coding and documentation. The Chilean fruit industry does now represent a viable opportunity for equipment companies able to assist the industry to mechanise, to automate, to harvest *fast* a growing but no less perishable fruit stock, to process, to pack and to ship it to the world's most discerning customers.

Far more often, however, we find that the reason for the failure of a new entrant into a market is the reason most often quoted for the defeat of great armies in battles through history, that of being 'too late'. This can apply, of course, to a company which is successful in a number of geographical markets with a particular product and yet has not entered other parts of the world where other companies have penetrated and established themselves. A

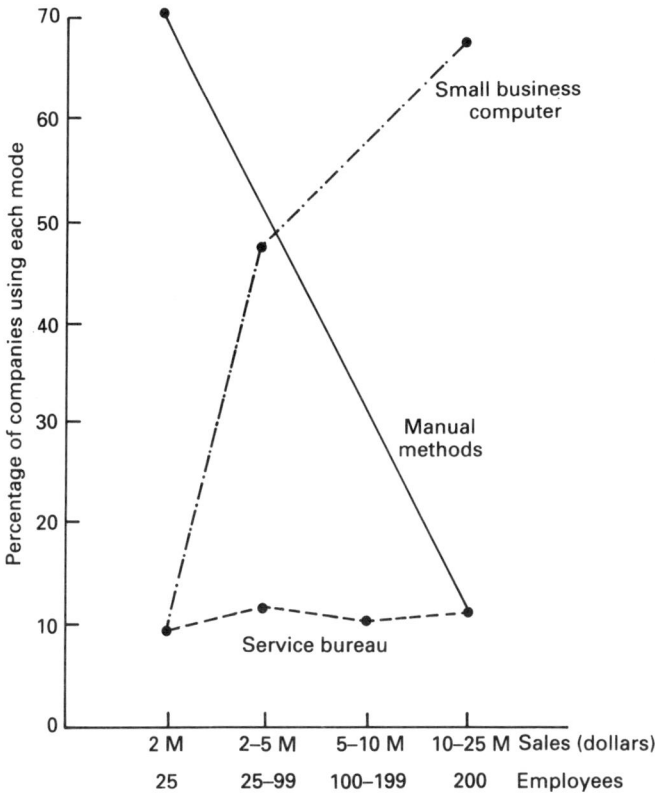

Figure 2.4 Use of personal computers in small business, 1981. This graph shows both growth and decline: growth in the use of the small business computer, but growth which clearly is seen to moderate; and steep decline in 'manual methods'. This, of course, is a real decline for the practitioners of manual methods and supporting industries and services.

move too late in the day to try and exploit such a geographical market can be not only frustrating but enormously costly in terms of investment, especially when, in order to justify the investment, management time is diverted away from those markets which had previously been successful.

For British companies most of the pitfalls of this kind seem to have arisen when attacking American markets. 'Too late' is not, of course, the only reason for the failure of British companies or companies importing from other nations to compete well in the USA. European and Japanese companies in the 1970s attempting to market plastic disposable blood-transfusion equipment in America spent enormous time and energy trying to get their business going, but the large American companies were so well established and the maturity of the market was such that without innovative products the European and Japanese entrants were literally 'too late'. They would have been better advised to use the time and energy in exploiting other international markets more aggressively. Paradoxically, this could have hurt the American producers strategically because they were also making every effort to expand internationally to build on the strong home positions which they had established but which were at that time showing declining growth due to maturity. For multinational and international companies the issue of global strategic thinking is extremely important.

COMPETITIVE PRESENCE AS A THREAT IN NEW MARKETS

Our discussion in the previous section leads us to some deeper consideration of this issue. All the market research may have been done and may show a very large market very responsive to a particular kind of product; the detailed marketing research which explores the future could show very attractive growth rates for a number of years to come. Pricing may be strong, margins high, but unless companies look very carefully at competitive presence in a market they feel to be attractive, investment, time and energy may be wasted and management tied up in a lost cause. Companies with high market share in large and profitable market areas will defend ferociously if a new entrant appears and threatens the business. In the USA and in Japan, in Germany, in all of the larger economies, strongly positioned home producers, who also happen to export to other countries, will go to great lengths to prevent a new competitor from gaining a foothold. So the small to medium-sized company which has a product with one or two interesting features should think very carefully before investing in the launching of such a product into a market dominated by an industry leader. A prime example of where we have seen the desperate cut and thrust of market-share protection is the computer industry. At a more basic level the electronics component industry, essentially much more of a commodity market and serving the computer industry, has also been subject to fierce price-cutting and even below-cost sale activities designed to protect an attractive business for the long term, to preserve world-wide capacity and jobs, or as part of an international strategy where a multinational may still remain profitable with a certain product line which is sold at much higher prices elsewhere.

Particular attention should be paid by British and other EC companies planning to do business in the USA and Japan. While freer trade and the breaking down of barriers is much spoken of and while progress is clearly being made, there are skills at play in those two great industrial nations which can make it extraordinarily difficult for the importing company, even with an outstanding product, to become established. It will be very interesting to see what impact the single European market has on this kind of dynamic, but whether it be the USA or Japan or whether it simply be the telecommunications industry in Britain or Europe, directors and management groups would be well advised to take a close look at competitive presence in any new market under study, and assess the threat of dominant competition to a proposed and possibly costly new market initiative.

THE DIRECTOR'S ROLE IN DECISIONS ON MARKET ASSESSMENTS, METHODOLOGY AND INVESTMENT

Obviously companies have a responsibility to themselves and their share-holders to optimise the use of the company's resources. Marketing and sales people are generally enthusiastic and optimistic, and so they should be. Competitive selling is a tough business and requires determination, panache, and a great deal of self-confidence. The director's role in enabling the company to reach the best possible decisions should be one of objectivity and incisiveness in the review and examination of information and proposals. Enthusiastic and ambitious sales and marketing managers must be forced to present properly structured business plans to complement good scientific market data and should literally be grilled and challenged so that at the end of the day the best possible decision is made. There will be opportunistic situations where all the data are just not available, but the optimism and ambition prevail. On such occasions the chairmen and directors will need to exercise judgement largely of an intuitive nature and here again the experience of the chairman or board member can be a decisive element in the fast, effective, business decision.

Whole volumes have been published on the subject of market identification, market and marketing research. This chapter has attempted to provide a practical guide and stimulus to thought of the busy chairmen or director confronting the process of exploration of potential markets. Specific volumes listed in the bibliography may be helpful to the reader wishing to delve further into these subjects.

CHAPTER 3

---------------------- ℧ ----------------------

CRITERIA FOR ASSESSING MARKET
ATTRACTIVENESS

It is important that we explore in a little more detail the criteria and the process whereby market attractiveness may be assessed and choices between available courses of action made. This chapter builds on Chapter 2 by looking at:

- Appropriateness to the company's business.
- Size and growth.
- Maturity and competitive structure.
- Assessing profit potential before entry.
- Exposures on receivables and currency movements.
- Available distribution channels and infrastructure.
- Special considerations with regard to the USA and Japan.
- Warning signs to look for.

APPROPRIATENESS TO THE COMPANY'S BUSINESS

Let us take a case from business life to examine this point. The Domino Group became a world leader in the marketing of an industrial ink-jet printing product for printing small codes on products such as beverage cans, milk cartons, and the like. While Domino was busy building an international business selling products to print this kind of code in a variety of industries, a significant number of other companies world-wide were developing and marketing a different kind of ink-jet printer which printed much larger characters mostly on cartons. When I joined the board of Domino at the end of 1984 a furious debate was in process as to whether Domino should enter the large-character carton-coding business or continue to focus on small-character printers only. There was a very clear division between those who said 'the large-character business is already sewn up; there are many competitors; the business isn't growing any more; we are too late', and those who claimed that 'our product line will not be complete without a large-character printer, and we don't want to stay a one-product company; having a large-character printer in the family is appropriate to our business'. Because a suitable large-character product became available for acquisition the company eventually decided to extend its range, even though the most vocal dissenters remained unconvinced. Although it was not clear at the time of the decision, the new Domino product, when eventually developed, did have certain unique features which made it attractive to particular customers and the exercise proved a success. At that time Domino was a young company but a form of crude product positioning did take place and this will be picked up when the case is discussed in a later chapter of the book. The point being emphasised here is that it is not always clear whether a new product or activity in a new market is appropriate to the company's business. The question must be asked, it must be debated, and facts must be produced wherever possible.

SIZE AND GROWTH

Size and growth may seem an obvious point to consider in a discussion of criteria for assessing market attractiveness. But the reality is that many companies do enter geographical or industrial market sectors without any data of this type. It must be said that the case of Domino entering the large-character printer market belonged in this category. There were no available hard data to show the size, value or trends in the market, though the company has now become more mature and capable at market assessment and the data exist.

In a world where resources are finite, the choice has to be made between proceeding or not in any given market, however defined. A simple rule to be applied in this situation should surely be that the proposer of any initiative to enter a new market, or even to do major exploration work, should be able to give at least some headline information on market size and growth and to translate this into business potential for the firm.

Deciding, in advance of gathering statistics, how to define 'size' of markets, is important. For a consumable product it is simply the volume which will be used or bought in a given period of time. For industrial equipment it is usual to look at both installed base and annual placements, together with the value of consumable business as calculated to develop over time.

Growth rates are often difficult to calculate, but in most fields historical trends will tell a great deal about consumer behaviour or industrial investment in certain types of manufacturing. In the case of a company like Domino, it is possible to gather information of a detailed kind showing where in the world different kinds of packaging lines exist, and to look at the trends in and future projections of annual installations of this type of equipment. Therefore it is possible to put a fairly reliable number on the likely growth in demand for industrial ink-jet printers by making assumptions about the numbers of existing and new packaging and production lines likely to install such equipment. These are the simple but important kinds of calculation which must be done in sales or marketing departments or by strategic planners and analysts to help management understand dimensions and growth rates or market opportunity.

Directors occupied in service industries also need to consider aspects of market size and growth as part of business planning. In any service-related company planning to grow substantially on an international basis, the dimension of international economic growth, differences in industrial growth in various parts of the world, and other broad factors will have to be taken into account. Consider the example of a company in the field of executive search. This is a London-based company which has grown a client base quickly and generated sufficient sales and profits and a team of consultants to the point where consideration is being given to where the most likely next profitable markets will be. This company confronts the same kinds of question as a company in the manufacturing industry which wishes to serve consumers in Europe or the broader world. You may say it will be obvious that certain European countries with expanding economies are the places to go. But if our London-based company needs to make choices and decide where the next tranche of investment should go, it will need to assess carefully the relative growth rates of industry in, for example, France, Spain, Italy and Germany; patterns of executive recruitment; the length of time executives spend with companies and whether (as in Japan) in any of those European countries mentioned, a concept of 'lifelong service' applies. We know that in some European countries there is a very great deal of executive movement as part of the process of individuals advancing their careers. In service industries just as in any other, understanding the market, assessing objectively where new markets are or might be, and prioritising to direct scarce resources into specific channels step by step, is a process which will have to be undertaken and firmly directed.

MATURITY AND COMPETITIVE STRUCTURE

In the last chapter we discussed the considerable threat which can exist to a new market entrant in either a monopoly or a market dominated by a strong home producer. Maturity, when applied to markets, is a very difficult concept. Sales people label the market 'mature' when their sales flatten off, often not seeing that this can be explained by the fact that the competition is taking the business rather than that demand is actually reducing. However, when assessing market attractiveness, it is essential to gather detailed information about the way in which an industry or a country market has grown over a period of time (if this is possible) and to have a very clear idea of the competitive structure. The number of competitors, the strategies they employ, whether they manufacture at home or are importers, the quality of their distribution, their financial viability, the dependence of their total business on the particular items in question – these are some of the questions that need to be answered in order to draw conclusions about the response of competition to a new entrant. This, of course, will again vary with the degree of maturity in a particular market. If a market is growing rapidly, with demand growing exponentially, a number of competitors can participate, all so busy following leads and filling orders that they will not be so concerned about the destruction of new entrants. In a more mature market like that described previously for blood transfusion equipment in the USA, the market leaders may be so well established and so dependent on the business and so well resourced to block any new entrant in a market not growing fast, that an attempt to enter that market could be futile. Maturity and competitive structure can be conveniently thought of in an integrated way. There is clearly a connection between them.

ASSESSING PROFIT POTENTIAL BEFORE ENTRY

Does your company assess profit potential before entry for either new products or new market initiatives? If so, please pass on to the next section!

Many companies entering new countries with their basic product range or entering a new industrial market with an existing product, or about to launch a new product into a variety of markets, do not have a structured profit plan or a calculation of the expected break-even point or rate of return over time. The management process should always include properly structured profit planning. The finance department is not the place where all such profit plans should be generated, though it is clearly a department which will take a great interest in such plans and should check the numbers.

Examples 3.1 and 3.2 show how chairman and directors might be presented with information on the profit potential of a proposal to enter a new market. Such a proposal might come from the director of marketing, the marketing manager or product manager.

There are various methods and companies often have individual approaches to carrying out this kind of work. The crucial point is that the process needs to be in place and designed so as to serve the needs of directors who will be the ultimate decision-makers on resource allocation.

Example 3.1 Profit Potential – Pre-Marketing Analysis

In this example, from Hardy (1962), we see two possible new products compared on a full costing basis, to show expected profit contribution in the first two years of sales.

	Total £	Product A £	Product B £
Year I			
Sales value	100,000	50,000	50,000
Direct cost	75,000	35,000	40,000
Overhead	20,000	10,000	10,000
	95,000	45,000	50,000
Net Profit	5,000	5,000	–
Year II			
Sales Value	150,000	100,000	50,000
Direct Cost	110,000	70,000	40,000
Overhead	24,000	16,000	8,000
	134,000	86,000	48,000
Net Profit	16,000	14,000	2,000

Example 3.2 New Product Marketing: Financial Plan And Analysis

This example, also from Hardy (1962), gives more detail and depth of analysis of the possible return on investment flowing from the launch of a new product.

John Graham Ltd have under consideration a proposal for a new product. A financial plan for the new product has been proposed and is set out below. Senior management are satisfied that the plan is the best one for the product, and they require guidance as to the percentage rate of return on investment the plan promises to bring forth.

The minimum rate of return the Company is prepared to consider is 15%. It is reasoned that the new product should assist certain of the existing products, and that this will balance its adverse effect on others.

Calculation of the percentage rate of return

A. *Discounted Cash Flow Approach*

(i) A present value is obtained for the minus contributions and the additional expenditure on plant and stocks during the earlier years.

Year	Proposed capital investments (£000's)	Present value of the capital investments proposed for the new product (discounted at 15%) (£000's)
0–1	250	232
1–2	260	208
2–3	110	76
3–4	40	24
		£540

(ii) The present value of contributions is discounted

	Contributions	Present value of contributions discounted at		
Year	(£000's)	20%	(£000's)	25%
0–1	–	–		–
1–2	–	–		–
2–3	–	–		–
3–4	–	–		–
4–5	230	94		75
5–6	270	90		68
6–7	320	87		63
7–8	320	72		49
8–9	370	68		44
9–10	320	48		30
10–11	290	36		21
11–12	245	24		14
12–13	195	16		9
13–14	160	11		5
14–15	110	6		3
		552		381

(iii) The percentage rate of return is calculated by interpolation.

	£		£
Present value at 20%	= 552	Present value at 20%	= 552
Present value of capital invested	= 540	Present value at 25%	= 381
Difference	12	Difference	171

Interpolating for the rate of return

$$= 20\% + \left(5\% \times \frac{12}{171} \right) = 20\cdot35\%$$

B. *Average Rate of Return Approach*

	£000's
Total contribution recieved over 15 years	= 2,620
Less allowance for depreciation of plant etc.	= 450
	2,170
Average contribution for year	145
Average capital invested 450 ÷ 2	= 225

$$\text{Percentage rate of return} = \frac{145}{225} \times \frac{100}{1} + 64\cdot44\%$$

C. *Pay back approach*

Contributions will equal outgoings after approx. 6¹/₂ years.

NOTE: In order to maintain simplicity, taxation has not been considered in this illustration.

The plant and machinery to be purchased for use in the manufacture of the product is not expected to have a residual value after 15 years of operation

New product financial plan

Year	1	2 £	3 £	4 £	5 £	6 £	7 £	8 £	9 £	10 £	11 £	12 £	13 £	14 £	15 £
Additional Sales	—	900	1100	1350	1500	1600	1600	1600	1500	1400	1200	1000	800	600	400
Additional raw material, package & direct labour	—	450	550	675	750	800	800	800	750	700	600	500	400	300	200
Additional manufacturing expenses	—	30	30	35	35	40	40	40	40	40	30	30	30	20	20
Additional advertising & promotion	—	600	600	500	450	450	400	400	300	300	250	200	150	100	50
Additional administration & other expenses	—	30	30	30	35	40	40	40	40	40	30	25	25	20	20
Total additions	—	1110	1210	1240	1270	1330	1280	1280	1130	1080	910	755	605	440	290
Additional contributions	—	−210	−110	110	230	270	320	320	370	320	290	245	195	160	110
Additional expenditure on plant stock holding, etc.	250	50		150											

EXPOSURES ON RECEIVABLE AND CURRENCY MOVEMENTS

This situation applies, of course, to exporters. Companies in the UK are being exhorted by the Department of Trade and Industry to concentrate more and more on exporting. World markets are very attractive for certain products. Some companies will not thrive if they do not find overseas markets because of the small size of the home market. However, exporting for export's sake is not a good thing, and by no means every company successful in the home market will become a successful exporter. There are so many factors, not least among them the market, the application of and demand for the product, and the capability of the company itself which may only be a producing company. There are examples of successful UK companies being led into the wilderness or towards ruin by rushing to export only to find that resources were soaked up in markets which were unresponsive. Some companies that succeeded in gaining sales and shipping large product volumes subsequently found that payment was not forthcoming, distributors were less than honest or went bankrupt, or that currency movements changed to such an extent that the translation of sales and profits into hard cash for consolidation into the accounts made a sad and sorry picture. It is important, therefore, when thinking about export markets to involve sufficiently knowledgeable members of the staff of financial departments to carry out the most rigorous of credit checks on overseas customers and distributors and also to work with expert advisers to gain at least some understanding of likely currency movements and the impact these will have on the home business, wherever this may be. It is, of course, possible to hedge on currency exposures and much depends upon the currency in which the billing is done if business is situated in the UK or USA. This matter is dealt with in more detail in Chapter 8 where we discuss working with distributors, dealers and trading partners. For insurance against overseas bad debts, Export Credit Guarantee Schemes are available and highly recommended.

AVAILABLE DISTRIBUTION CHANNELS AND INFRASTRUCTURE

Clearly, when assessing the attractiveness of a market the availability of skilled people, be they likely employees or distributors and dealers, is a crucial issue. In most developed countries it is a straightforward matter to gain information on methods of distribution and available trading partners. However, in some Asian and Latin American countries it is not so easy to gain ready assessments of available and preferred channels of distribution and technical support for certain kinds of product. When making decisions on where to go, in terms of new market exploitation choices, this is a most important issue and will be dealt with in more detail later in the book.

USA AND JAPAN – SPECIAL CONSIDERATIONS

Any European company aiming to enter either of these great markets or industry sectors within them would be wise to carry out very extensive market and competitive research. The distribution system in Japan is many-layered and it is impossible in some business sectors to operate without using it. The route of a direct operation is also more difficult in Japan and many companies start with a distributor and move to a joint venture, and in some cases eventually become independent. In the USA there exists an outstanding distribution system for many products which can be tapped into readily with the right product and the right local trading partner. In both the USA and Japan market leaders in many businesses tend to be strong American or Japanese companies. They are often financially solid, extremely resourceful, have large direct operations and/or tap into distribution channels and are often ready to invest significant amounts of money in maintaining market share. Companies in Europe buying into America through acquisitions have often run into difficulties. Directing and managing businesses in America or Japan from Europe is not an easy matter. The sheer geography is a very large hurdle. Despite all these reservations, success can be achieved, and many British companies which have early problems in the USA do succeed in growing profitable businesses in these important areas. The point being made here is that, when assessing the attractiveness of markets, simply to look at size and growth rates would be a potential recipe for catastrophe.

WARNING SIGNS TO LOOK FOR

Company directors should focus attention on warning signs at the point of assessment of market attractiveness. It is well to be wary of expansive words and enthusiasm from marketing people not backed by data. High inflation rates and unstable economies do not generally represent a good start for an export business. If any market, be it geographical or an industry sector, is dominated by a small number of large companies located in the country or countries in question, and if the product or service to be marketed is in no way unique or particularly innovative, it is quite in order to hesitate and challenge the proposal. If the market is declining, clearly further questions will need to be asked, and unless trading partners can be recommended on the basis of proven credit-worthiness, it is unwise to sign distribution agreements in a hurry. If the proposer of the initiative cannot produce a three-year financial assessment and market potential, it would be unwise to approve the plan.

CONCLUSION

The overall point of emphasis in all of this is that the chairman and fellow directors have an important role to play in ensuring that an overall structure is in place which enables appropriate assessment of opportunities against defined criteria. Many a presentation has been argued on the basis that 'it was strategically important'. Any move proposed which is strategically important for any kind of company, must surely be backed by an assessment of the profit or return on investment which will accrue. Strategy in business is aimed primarily at profit generation and profit improvement. A 'strategic programme' should surely be, over time, the most profitable of any.

CHAPTER 4

***

SELECTING AND PRIORITISING NEW MARKET OPPORTUNITIES AND DEVELOPING AN OVERALL PLAN

In earlier chapters we have taken a close look at the importance of identifying customers and understanding their decision criteria; of developing a nomenclature and an understanding of new markets, categorising them and at least having some formal approach to deciding what and where a new market might be; and then in Chapter 3 we looked at some of the criteria which can be applied to assess market attractiveness.

We are now reaching a point where we may be receiving a quantity of hard data and we may even feel we are beginning to be confronted with choices. Let us assume that we are the directors of an industrial equipment company which has certain technological expertise and which has an established range of products which have been reasonably successful across a limited spectrum of markets. Our goal is growth, and we now begin to confront the complexities outlined in earlier chapters of the book related to available markets and difficult investment decisions. How can we begin to think about allocating scarce resources to exploit specific prospects if we are confronted with an array of opportunities and different opinions?

In order to prioritise new market opportunities and develop an overall plan a structured approach is essential. In order to decide where to go next, a variety of courses of action will probably be under consideration. The logical pathway will be to review where we are, and to look at the prospects and the facts (if any) which back them up. It should not be surprising that the issue of deciding on exploration and exploitation of new markets is essentially a strategic review process.

The logical steps in the model process we would now discuss are as follows:

1. Assemble relevant facts.
2. Consult the 'experts', both in-house and external, in order to check the facts and gain advice and suggestions on how they might be used.

3. Model possible pathways and outcomes – test the water.
4. Formulate a clear overall strategy (not too much detail will be necessary at this stage).
5. If partnerships, acquisitions or other kinds of alliance are involved in the evolving strategy or options, early due diligence to investigate the quality of partners or acquisition candidates will be needed.
6. Build a structure to enable final decisions to be taken. The decisions need to be incisive, and plans and follow-up will need to proceed from this point to create appropriate action and results.

Let us work our way through the model stage by stage.

GATHERING FACTS

By the time we reach this point in the process we will have an enormous amount of data to hand. These will be statistical data, business data and also human data, for example the views and opinions of a variety of people. The process of structuring information and pulling appropriate data together which are going to be relevant to discussion and decisions is something which takes time and requires a skill which should not be underestimated. If we are looking at a variety of options then the data need to be presented in a summary form; an example is represented in Figure 4.1. For each of the options described in Figure 4.1 back-up data will be available, again in summary form, and could be presented as laid out in Example 4.1

Example 4.1 Data Describing/Proposing Strategic Option

France

Taking one of the examples shown in Figure 4.1 – for directors to consider supporting a proposal to take their business into France, by forming a subsidiary or using a distributor, would involve them in seeking detailed information. The data expected from the project sponsor would need to be carefully structured and should cover:

1. The French market
   (a) Size – units and value
   (b) Growth – history and projections
   (c) Competitive structure and market shares
   (d) Regulatory/legislative/environmental issues

Option	Rationale	Immediate Mid or Long Term	Sponsor	Resource Requirement	Comments and next steps
Geographical 1. Expansion a. France b. Italy c. Japan Full line – all products entry	) * World's fastest growing markets for product X.) * Competitors already active) * Many enquiries	) All immediate but we will be stretched to do all at once.	a. Joe Black, European Marketing Director b. Alan Drew, Chairman c. Jane Smith, Export Sales Manager	a. Acquisition – major finances and manpower b. Minor c. Moderate financial, major manpower	a. Acquisition option or distributorship for France b. Italy – excellent distributor candidate c. Japan – possible joint venture *Data* suggest Italy 'ready to go'. France and Japan need detailed business plan and 5 year P&L. *Action* – Final Plan for Italy. Business plans to board for France and Japan

Figure 4.1 Strategic options for new market entry

Option	Rationale	Immediate Mid or Long Term	Sponsor	Resource Requirement	Comments and next steps
2. Enter UK pharmaceutical market with existing range	New legislation under Medicines Act has created significant demand	Immediate or mid-term. Long term will *miss* time window	Bill Higgins, Market Development Manager	* Financial – 2 new sales positions, i.e. new Product Manager and Promotional Campaign * Manpower, Director would need to oversee programme	Marketing finance directors to review Higgins' business plan and range 3–5 year profit. Goals against France/ Japan options.

Figure 4.1 Strategic options for new market entry (Continued)

2. The subsidiary option
    (a) Overall plan
    (b) 3–5-year financial projections
    (c) Start of investment
    (d) Proposed organisation
    (e) Facilities proposal
    (f) Timing of proposed actions
    (g) Risks and opportunities

3. The distributor route plan
    (a) Available distributors and assessment of each
        (i)   business issues
        (ii) financial
        (iii) examination
    (b) Competitor business methods and details
        (i)   direct?
        (ii) distributor national?
        (iii) French companies?
    (c) Costs associated with distributorship
    (d) 3–5-year financial projections for distributor approach

4. Commentary and recommendations
    (a) Financial comparison of options
    (b) Other comparisons and factors

5. Recommendation and rationale

Summary facts of this kind, together with commentary, should be circulated to those who are going to be involved in any decision process to allow adequate time for study and consideration. Such information should certainly be presented before any meetings are called to debate or discuss such data. Sometimes a good technique is to call a meeting at which the data are presented and to have those who have compiled the data go over them and ensure that all recipients have a clear understanding of the purpose of the data and give the opportunity for questions about the information and the proposals themselves. All of this should be done *before* the strategic discussion proper, thus giving time for thought and consideration after the initial briefing. It is often helpful to have information presented in this way rather than simply to receive it in the mail.

CONSULTING EXPERTS

Once we have reached a point of summarising a series of objectives it can be helpful to talk to marketing and business people holding specialist positions in the company, and also to seek the thoughts and advice of external, and therefore independent, experts. This also serves as a useful check on some of the information and assertions which will have been compiled in presenting directors with options and proposals for new market initiatives.

Some companies adopt the process with all significant investment programmes of involving a known and trusted outside company of consultants. If the consultants have the right relationships and have built a good rapport with sufficient managers inside the organisation, this process can work well. If the outside consultants are seen effectively as 'judges' of inside work, or 'second guessers' then the result can be negative and a sour atmosphere may develop. Chairmen and directors need to think of these issues carefully in organising the process of selecting and prioritising new market opportunities.

MODELLING POSSIBLE OUTCOMES

It can be extremely helpful if management services departments, executive assistants or line management are able to build a 'what if?' model, to put meat on the bones of a bare proposal to enter a new market. With the computer power now available to us all it takes no great effort to develop outline business plans for specific options, and such programmes are used more and more often in the boardroom not only for hard-copy presentations but also to enable examination of questions on the plan. It would not be advisable to agree to a new market initiative without being presented with a simple business plan which tracks over a number of years into the future. It is also useful to see some data and a forward model based on a decision 'not to do what is proposed'. In other words, to examine what would be the negative impact of not taking the new market initiative proposed.

There are many options available these days to enable the modelling of possible outcomes of new market initiatives to be a meaningful exercise. In Example 4.2 an example is given of the summary overview of a model which has been to show the potential to a certain company (a real company) in entering a new market area with an entirely new product. This model, although incomplete, enabled directors to see that the proposers of a scheme had thought things through and that on face value at least there was clearly a market present and a definite profit potential for exploiting it in a certain way.

Example 4.2 Modelling new market entry

Product 'BB' had elements of new technology. It was seen both as a replacement for 'older technology' and, because it had new and unique features, it was expected to create entirely new opportunities as well.

Market for BB in UK, France, Germany, Netherlands and Italy, 1989–92

	1989	1990	1991	1992
Total units of BB type product	1,000	1,500	2,250	3,150
Value (£ thousands)	2,000	3,000	4,500	6,300
BB units	300	750	1,750	2,500
Share of total (%)	30	50	78	79
BB value (£ thousands)*	600	1,500	3,500	5,000
BB consumables value	100	300	700	1,000

*Proposed unit selling price of BB £2,000

4-Year Profit Plan (£ thousands)

	1989	1990	1991	1992
Total sales	700	1,800	4,200	6,000
Gross margin	315	810	1,764	2,400
Operating expenses	300	450	575	750
Profit contribution	15	360	1,189	1,650
Return on sales	2.1%	20	28 %	28 %

- Sales and Market Share estimates considered conservative.
- Sales through distributors/dealers: no direct sales force cost.
- Very low service cost, user-friendly product.

Comment

This looks like a highly attractive investment/new market option. Directors presented with this type of data would be wise to challenge strongly on:

- Validity of market size and growth assumptions.
- Feasibility of 'BB' products achieving the projected market share penetration. Is the sales forecast believable? What does the product have that the competition lacks? Serious questions would be necessary on this point.
- Where are the increasing operating expenses going?

Unless product 'BB' has unique features, a 'special' price or our company has a team of super salespeople, this looks like a highly ambitious plan and yet, if it comes off, it will clearly be a winner.

Attention to detail in the review given will be necessary.

FORMULATING A STRATEGY

If a board or a group of directors has been through the process of selecting a number of new market initiatives to pursue, it will be necessary to prioritise these in terms of business potential and the way in which resources and organisation are to be developed in order to ensure that initiatives can be carried through. This process, layered on to an existing business, will effectively bring about an adjustment or a radical change in overall corporate strategy. Once a number of new market initiatives have been decided upon and prioritised, the strategic importance of these plans will need to be compared with that of other plans and activities within the company; the revised strategy, including the new market strategy, should then be clearly expressed and prepared for communication to the management groups within the company and indeed all employees who will need to be involved. The clear communication and common understanding of what has been decided and what is to be done are critical aspects of moving from strategy into action planning and the achievement of results.

DUE DILIGENCE ON POSSIBLE PARTNERS OR ACQUISITIONS

Moving into the planning phase, any new market initiatives which involve third parties, partners, acquisitions or ventures, will need to be preceded by very careful 'due diligence'. Companies making acquisitions will always go through the process of financial 'due diligence' where a firm of auditors will examine in great detail all aspects of financial performance and financial projections of the target acquisition company.

However, experience shows that other kinds of 'due diligence' are advisable before making acquisitions, collaborating or entering ventures. This activity could include an audit of the customers of the partner or acquisition candidate to see whether they are satisfied with the products and services they receive and whether indeed those products function well in the field. The sales force of target companies should also be interviewed by independent bodies to gain a clear view of their feelings and judgements of the products, services and performance of their company. If the company concerned is an engineering operation or involved in technology, specialist consulting firms can take a very close look at the engineering competence of the firm or the technology which is on offer. A world-wide network of consultants and expert advisers exists and can be tapped. Investments in this kind of exploration are usually money well spent. Investigations may lead to the abandonment of particular projects but in many instances will raise issues and questions for the host company which at least provide directors with a more objective view of what may be entailed in going ahead. It is easier to take a decision and go ahead with some objective information indicating problem areas that will have to be tackled.

The history of recent business activities of UK companies involving US acquisitions is littered with examples of the bitter disappointment which can result from a failure to take proper account of the need for 'due diligence'. One fairly recent example of a US acquisition going very badly wrong concerned a highly successful British company in the industrial equipment business. This had proceeded through its first few years of life to become a well-respected public company with a distributor in the USA which had been given some limited capability under licence to produce locally. After two years of US manufacture the licensee had built up a reasonable business with a significant number of installations across North America. The UK company had not controlled carefully the way in which the licensee was able to modify equipment. Equipment was reaching customers which suffered from technical problems which made it unreliable, especially when compared to the UK company's first class products on sale all over Europe. Eventually the UK company acquired its US licensee and although it went through all the usual processes of 'due diligence' from a financial point of view, it was unable to detect before the acquisition significant customer disenchantment and technical problems in the field. Since the licensee had built up a business quickly, the sales and profits achieved were attractive. But soon after the acquisition chickens came home to roost and the UK company found that it had acquired a disillusioned customer base and a company fast gaining a bad reputation in the USA. The emergence of additional competitive companies in the USA coincided with the discoveries made by the UK company of the problems it had acquired, and for a period of three years significant investments were needed to set matters straight during which time the profitability of the US acquisition was extremely disappointing. This had the effect of causing a significant rerating of the value of the group by investors and analysts and also required a very great deal of management time since the US company underwent a complete restructuring, with the entire local management group being replaced.

This is not an unusual example, and brings into focus a particularly important question directors should ask when acquiring any business, particularly one located three or four thousand miles away: 'If this business is so successful and so profitable, why are the sellers getting out?' If, as in the example quoted, the sellers are not to be involved in the business after the acquistion, such questions assume an even greater significance. If the sellers intend to stay on and manage the business, directors of any company in any country making an acquisition, particularly those buying an overseas company, should consider very seriously using a formula for buying the business which relates the eventual amount paid to the profit result achieved over time. This 'earn-out' approach is becoming increasingly common and has a very great deal to recommend it. If a selling principal can achieve 40 or 50 per cent more in price for the business he is selling by staying on and producing a certain level of performance he may well be inspired to do so.

FINAL DECISIONS, COMMUNICATION AND FOLLOW-UP

At the end of all the discussion and examination there will be final decisions. These may be positive or negative, and it is important that the chairman or board communicate decisions clearly, not only to those who will be directly involved in implementation but also to the whole of the organisation – in the case of a public company, to investors and the public at large. It goes without saying that the follow-up to a positive decision is to take action. The board would normally follow up by reviewing subsequent actions and checking that delegated authority to get things done is properly used. One of the main roles of the chairman and the board, especially in companies that have grown to substantial size, beyond the obvious processes of decision and investment, should be to pay proper attention to the communication processes company-wide so that an organisation moves forward to exploit new market opportunities in the full knowledge of all employees and with their support and also with the support and understanding of investors.

CHAPTER 5

⎯⎯⎯⎯⎯⎯⎯⎯⎯⎯ ⌒ ⎯⎯⎯⎯⎯⎯⎯⎯⎯⎯

NEW MARKETS AND 'NEW' AND 'OLD' PRODUCTS

Terminology in business can be loose. We have already discussed the difficulty in deciding what a 'new' product or a 'new' market is. It is worth reiterating here that a 'new' market needs to be defined in the individual company context. A new market to one company may not be 'new' in the innovative sense at all. It may simply be a market that the company has not previously tackled.

It is useful to reflect in a similar way on products. An 'old' product in one market can be seen very much as 'new' in territories which have not seen it before or market sectors into which it has not been launched.

These points are made simply to emphasise the reality that new product marketing and new market initiatives are not confined to strictly innovative product offerings. The techniques of introducing an 'old' product into a 'new' market sector will be very similar to new-product marketing techniques used to introduce an entirely innovative product. Because a product has succeeded in one market sector or one geographical area it should not be assumed that the product will automatically enjoy the same level of acceptance elsewhere. This is a fallacy on which many unfortunate optimistic forecasts of unfulfilled business growth have been made. Exploiting a 'new' market with an extraordinary 'old' product requires as much thought and planning as an entirely innovative exercise and directors need to be on their guard against complacency or drawing the wrong conclusions from previous experience based on data compiled from a different market.

It is important at this stage to consider the issue of new product development as it relates to new and old products and the activities of competition. In most industrial fields a significant amount of money is likely to be spent on research and development in order to develop new products and gain a competitive advantage. In industrial marketing, and especially in high-technology businesses, competitors seek day by day, week by week, month by month, to gain an advantage by developing a superior device.

Add-ons, enhancements, upgrades, new software, the constant evolution of more and more complex and comprehensive products is a characteristic of high-technology business. The evolution of competitive devices in this kind of business can have an undue influence on the research and development focus and investment of a company. There is a tendency among sales and marketing people to 'cry wolf' about the way in which competitive hardware and software are being enhanced and to call frequently for parallel or greater upgrades in their own products. This can lead to virtually the whole of the company's activity being diverted and diluted into add-ons and enhancements while the really important process of planning and developing the next generation of products and the quantum leap in technology can be ignored or slowed down.

Service industries also need to keep product development and a concept of 'providing a complete product' under review. Airlines are a good relevant example. Competition for the business trade among airlines in Europe and world-wide is great. We have seen a battle over recent years in the business class/club class category. At the time of writing British Airways appears to be winning this battle, along with airlines such as SAS and Swissair in Europe. The product offered to the business traveller is no longer limited to better food, better wine, pre-assignment of seats, bigger seats, late check-in, and so on. It extends to things like free parking at the airport, a low-cost valet service for the passenger's car, banking arrangements, business centres and more comprehensively staffed executive lounges. In service industries in particular, understanding the needs and the psychology of the potential customer and finding ways of reaching him or her to communicate new product developments all represent particular challenges. After all, industrial products are mostly sold by warm-bodied salesmen calling on customers. The choice as to which airline ticket I buy is a very personal one and is based more on my current experiences and what I might read. No direct salesman confronts me with a presentation on 'here's why you should travel BA'.

INCREASING A PRODUCT'S PROFITABLE LIFE

The profitable life of a product may be increased by launching it in new countries, regions or industry sectors and by increasing penetration. This needs to be approached in a thorough way. In a high-technology company, core products which are proven in Western Europe, the USA and Japan, can be given an extra stimulus to the life cycle by being launched in new countries, especially those where competitors have not shown themselves to be strong. I was recently in South America exploring possibilities for Domino's established (i.e. 'old') products and found the soil effectively virgin. By entering certain

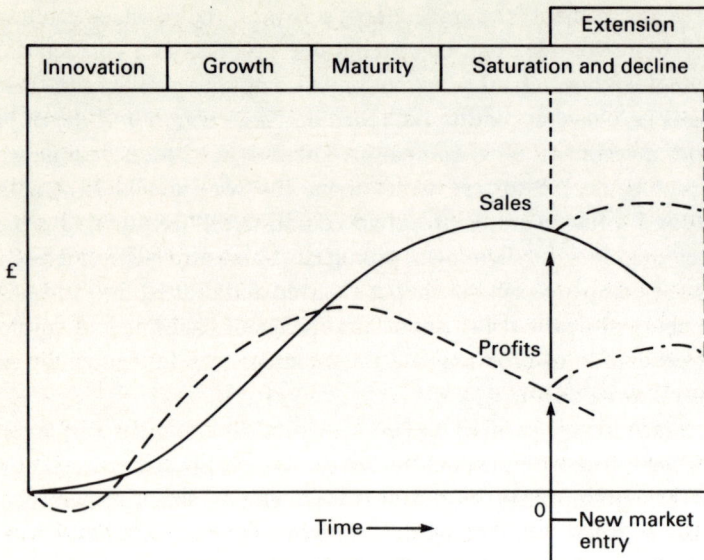

Figure 5.1 Extending the product life cycle. Here again is the classical product life cycle discussed earlier in the book. It shows the effect of launching the product in previously untapped South American markets. A similar 'positive tale of sales and profit growth' can also be achieved by enhancing or updating product features to gain more competitive sales in existing markets.

countries in South America the company's world-wide product sales could be significantly improved and the product life cycle extended, as illustrated in Figure 5.1. Even in markets which appear to be mature, if a company or product has not penetrated certain segments it is possible again to mount a new marketing initiative to increase penetration and again extend the life cycle of the product. It may be that some relatively modest technological enhancement is required to enable this to happen. A further example of major business growth in the printing and publishing industry was brought about by the application of specialised resources and the development of special computer control equipment to enable the interface of ink-jet printers with complex printing presses and magazine production equipment. The ink-jet printer products themselves were not in any sense new, but major new sales growth was generated and the product cycle extended for a number of years by a new market initiative based on good solid research and some peripheral technological innovation.

ENHANCING 'OLD' PRODUCTS

Product development in most companies involves the upgrading and enhancement of existing products and the parallel concentration on creative work to evolve an entirely new generation of products to serve different markets or to replace ultimately obsolete existing technology and product ranges. The enhancement of 'old' products is a very useful activity, especially for those products which are clearly identified as 'cash cows' within a company. The small innovations that make a medical product easier to use or enable a personal computer to have an extended range of performance or new software are examples of the enhancement of 'old' products. The 'new' flavours we see being made available for instant desserts, the upgrading of British Airways Super Club to provide travellers with more champagne and a choice of fine wines are further examples of the extension of life cycles of 'old' products with a view to improving competitive positioning or growing market share. The reader can probably think of many more examples. In Japanese industrial circles, especially in discussion of the Japanese quality concept, there is much talk of *Kaizen*. This word is roughly translated into English as 'to improve or make better' (*kai*) 'on a continuing basis' (*zen*). In other words, small steps added together over a period of time either enhance quality or make a product more valuable or of greater utility to the customer. We should not in any sense write off the importance of this sort of incremental improvement, and I contend that 'old' product enhancement is for many companies as important as the development of entirely new products.

DEVELOPING 'NEW' PRODUCTS

By using the terminology 'old' and 'new' product development, I have sought to distinguish between the enhancement and progress which can be made from an existing base and the truly innovative forward movement that arises when an entirely new product is created to serve a newly identified market or an entirely new product is designed in order to replace a range of products already available for an established purpose. 'New' product development of this kind is, of course, a much higher-risk business than enhancing what has already been proved successful. It requires a very great deal of support in terms of market research, customer motivational research and, once the action begins, attention to detail in multi-functional new product planning. The gap between defining a market need and planning a product to meet it is often very great indeed. Many examples have been quoted over the years in the literature of enormous amounts of money being expended on designing and developing new products which were complete failures. Perhaps the most often quoted is that of the Ford Edsel motor car.

The Ford Motor Company had expended a very great deal of time and energy analysing trends in the motor-car market and launched their new product in 1958. There was a general feeling among the public that the Edsel was the most researched new product ever to be introduced. However, what was clearly lacking upon detailed analysis was proper customer-based research on the concept and the product. *Business Week* (18 April 1964, p. 96) explains further what happened to the Edsel:

During the 1958 Automobile Model Year, it became clear to the Ford Motor Company, and shortly afterwards to everyone in the country, that the Edsel, the first new nameplate introduced to the US public by a major automobile company in twenty years, was a monumental failure. In the recriminations and publicity that followed, two aspects of Ford's planning were most criticised: the styling and the marketing research. The Edsel may have been no beauty, but cars rated as much worse aesthetic horrors sold just fine. *Missing* – the research which is something else again. The criticism was wide of the mark, because in any meaningful sense no marketing research was done on the Edsel. Ford men admit that the guts of the planning was 'market analysis' and the difference between that and research is crucial. Analysis is a review of an historical situation.

RESEARCH AND PRODUCT DEVELOPMENT

Among the most difficult functions to position in a company are research and product development. We are speaking of functions which will be staffed largely by creative engineers and scientists. In many research and development departments the average age is low. Many of the people involved are young graduates who are still in the process of learning how to work with others, and development work and research is full of uncertainty, pitfalls, problems and disappointments. It is also true to say that in many companies, particularly industrial companies, the marketing function is less than well developed, and therefore understanding of customer requirements, competitive offerings, and the options available for directing R & D resources are not clear. New product planning is one of the most difficult activities to organise effectively in industrial companies. Effective new product planning requires, among other things, the involvement of perceptive marketing people, creative development engineers, open-minded production people, quality assurance experts and good financial management. Bringing all of these activities together in order to implement good new product planning also requires leadership at the general management level. Processes for gathering market information, for exploring new product ideas, for brainstorming and distilling product strategies and discrete and well-defined new product designs and plans, are very hard to bring into being. This subject is explored in great detail in the next chapter.

Research and product development are in many fields the crucial issues in maintaining competitive advantage and the way in which R & D is structured and financed can be the critical factor in the success or failure of a company. And yet the structure and positioning of R & D must be done in such a way that it fits the overall strategy of the company and is focused on customers and markets and not on technology and scientists who would love to do nothing but pure research. In the business context pure research and technology evaluation are important but *managed* research is essential for any commercial company with limited resources.

In many companies the ultimate success of the research and development division depends upon the skill and professionalism of the marketing department or the product planning department, if such a speciality function exists.

CHAPTER 6

❦

MARKET DEVELOPMENT AND PRODUCT DEVELOPMENT

BALANCING THE APPROACH

Companies aim at 'business development'. They seek to optimise return on investment over time. In many instances public companies seek to produce a short- or medium-term profit result which will retain the support of shareholders. Fully integrated manufacturing and marketing companies, in addition to the obvious capital and resource investment in producing goods, will be carrying the larger part of other overhead costs in those expenses related to developing markets or developing new products. The balancing of investment is extremely difficult to plan and implement. The balance of investment between particular developments and of the evolution of new products for launch in one to one-and-a-half years is one issue. The longer-term strategic decisions on allocating funds for products which will not impact on the company's business for three, five or ten years are even more difficult.

One of the most difficult problems confronting directors seeking to allocate scarce resources wisely in the development of new products, may not be the competence of the research and development director or his staff. It is more likely to be the quality of definition of the next generations of a product, which is essentially the responsibility of marketing and general management.

The allocation of resources in order further to develop profitable sales of existing products rather than to generate entirely new products, can sometimes yield extraordinarily positive results. All of which should cause us to reflect back on earlier chapters in which we discussed issues such as markets, market maturity, market growth and increasing sales.

USING EXISTING PRODUCTS TO DEVELOP UNDEREXPLOITED MARKETS

Before investing significant new funds in new product development, directors could profitably examine ways in which existing products can add to the profit yield of a company by the development of new geographical markets or market sectors into which their particular products have yet to be sold. In many industries the kind of equipment manufactured by companies such as Domino Printing Sciences plc has penetrated to a level of less than 10 per cent of all of those production lines on which such equipment might be used. Particularly in the field of industrial marketing, the alternative of spending more money on marketing existing products into new market sectors or niches should be considered as well as allocating more resources to the development of entirely new products. Extraordinary opportunities for products occur in the most unlikely places. For instance, the use of industrial ink-jet printers at sea on trawlers is becoming fairly common. The larger trawlers stay at sea for long periods of time and are essentially fish-processing factories. The fish are caught, cleaned, gutted and packed so that when the trawler arrives on the quayside in the dock lorries are waiting to take the fresh produce directly to market. The availability of equipment which can operate in the relatively unstable environment of the trawler at sea, but which can mark and identify packets and boxes of fish and do so at low temperatures, has meant that a market niche has opened up for an industrial overprinting product which many imaginative directors would never have stumbled upon. Proper research and a constant scanning of industrial uses of equipment can bring about the potential for market exploitation with existing products which is far more profitable than spending the same amount of money on additional new product development.

WHEN IS PRODUCT DEVELOPMENT NEEDED?

This is an intriguing question. One could quote numerous examples of products which have survived for many years and remained market leaders without any significant investment in development. Such survivors include basic equipment for distillation produced on an industrial scale by companies like Manesty and certain kinds of mechanical equipment for handling documents in mailing houses which are used to insert letters and forms into envelopes. In both cases these industries have been growing and while some development may have been required to keep up with the pace of the introduction of computers and need for mechanical equipment to interface with them, the basic products appear very much as they did a number of years ago. This applies to consumer and industrial products. However, in most competitive fields (a good example would be the motor industry) product development is required not to produce a quantum leap in technology or an entirely new kind of motor car but to produce a new model which can be marketed in an appealing way, and either maintain or gain market share for the developer. In industrial fields, where much emphasis is placed on trade shows and the demonstration of equipment, innovation and 'new sizzle for the salesmen to sell' are considered to be important factors even when the eventual 'new' product is hardly new at all. Innovation, attractiveness, and new features (even if minor) which gain the attention of the potential buyer, have all become part of the quest for product enhancement and product development.

Companies operating in chosen consumer or industrial fields which succeed and sustain positions of leadership over time can generally be observed to be close to customers. Therefore, while there is no definitive answer to the question 'When is product development needed', it is clear that commercial companies in the industrial world seek competitive advantage and therefore will think of product-development needs relative to profitable growth, market share leadership and the obvious environmental and industrial trends discussed in earlier chapters. However, life can be difficult and confusing for directors confronted with significant investment proposals based on perceived needs for new products when there may be suspicions that the existing product range has not been well marketed, and the new product requests may be founded on the shifting sand of the apparent inability of sales and marketing staff to compete by selling an essentially sound existing product.

SALESFORCE TRAINING AND EFFECTIVENESS

If the directors of a company cannot feel assured that the salesforce and the marketing group working with today's product are fully effective and well trained and that requests for new products are well researched, the decision process will be difficult indeed. It is therefore a prerequisite of establishing processes whereby market development and product development can be properly considered by a board, to ensure that salesforce effectiveness and the training of sales people, understanding of markets and the company's progress within them, are well managed. These are functions which can be organised and run effectively and which can be subject to simple measures which boards can assess.

MARKETING PLANNING

The co-ordination of all of those activities which eventually result in effective presentation of products or services, advertising and sales promotion, and direct selling can be referred to as 'marketing planning'. Planning, of course, must lead to effective implementation so the correct terminology should perhaps be 'marketing planning and market implementation'. These are functions rarely performed effectively in many industrial companies. Consumer companies, with their extremely heavy emphasis on brand management and their substantial advertising budgets, present perhaps a more straightforward challenge. Whatever a company's business, and this includes service industries, a structured approach to marketing planning can only be helpful. A marketing plan for a group of products and for individual products, or for a geographical market or for products within a market, should be constructed by the responsible manager. This should state the overall intentions the company has in that market; from this a short list of key objectives can be distilled, and a detailed description drawn up of tasks needing to be implemented. Much has been written on the subject of marketing planning. It is essentially a technical process and requires the same kind of attention to detail that is seen in major project management throughout industry, and indeed in the planning and implementation of any significant new product development. Establishing marketing planning and implementation as living realities in a company can make a world of difference to marketing and sales effectiveness and ultimate profitability. A simple marketing planning process might be structured as in Example 6.1.

Example 6.1 Key Elements in Marketing Planning and the
Marketing Plan

1. The market

   (a) Market *definition*: what is the market?
   (b) Market *analysis* by geographical area and total:
       (i)   size;
       (ii) growth;
       (iii) value.
   (c) Market *structure*:
       (i)   competitors;
       (ii) market shares;
       (iii) trends in share movement.
   (d) Perceived market *gaps*.
   (e) Projected trends in
       (i) environment;
       (ii) legislation;

(iii) consumer behaviour;

(iv) manufacturing or other technology and methodology.

2. Strategic goal in entering the market

   (a) Overall *aims and objectives*: what and where do we want to be in this market?

   (b) *Market share* objectives over time.

   (c) *Market and product positioning*: where will we place ourselves relative to customers' competition and what will be our 'sales and marketing platform'?

   Headline financial goals for years 1–3:

   (i) sales;

   (ii) expenses;

   (iii) profits.

3. Detailed marketing plan

This will include a flow chart or Gantt chart, and more complex plans will of course be done these days on a personal computer. Directors will want to ensure the following elements are incorporated:

   (a) Detailed product plan backed by product specification.

   (b) Preparation of market plan and timetable – parallel to the R&D new product development plan.

   (c) Market introduction plan:

      (i) where and when;

      (ii) timetable by territory or country.

   (d) Sales forecast by territory or country by quarter beyond launch, years 1, 2 and 3.

   (e) Promotional plan and launch plan:

      (i) promotional strategy;

      (ii) campaign messages;

      (iii) types of promotional material and events, which could include exhibitions, conferences, trade advertising, public relations, literature, radio, TV, and other media, (including video);

      (iv) research plan to test promotional effectiveness: consumer interviews, user panels, questionnaires, analysis of leads generated;

      (v) promotional budget.
- (f) Salesforce, distributor and agents' training programme.
- (g) Technical training plans for a technical product.
- (h) Customer training programmes and materials including user guides and maintenance manuals.
- (j) Marketing project *team*:
  - (i) full-time and part-time members;
  - (ii) specific responsibilities.
- (k) Financial objectives of the plan by quarter and for years 1–3:
  - (i) sales;
  - (ii) gross profits;
  - (iii) expenses;
  - (iv) profit contribution;
  - (v) ratios such as return on sales.
- (l) Report and review structure:
  - (i) planned report frequency;
  - (ii) report format, including charts/graphs.
- (m) Significant opportunities to exceed plan and risks of problems.

PRODUCT PLANNING

Companies can be regional, national, or international on whatever scale. For companies which have traditionally enjoyed the greater part of business activity in the home country, and even for some that have spread a little further afield, product planning runs the risk of becoming somewhat local and parochial. Product planning is also one of the most difficult functions to establish appropriately in any company.

It may be helpful to think of the model of a medium-sized company – with, say, a turnover of £30 million – operating in the industrial equipment field and based in the UK. This company can serve a very wide spectrum of industry in numerous countries. It has enjoyed a reasonable export record over the years because it has operated in a market without too many competitors. Its thinking may essentially be focused on the United Kingdom and limited European requirements. This company may be operating in an industry where international markets are opening up, where North American and continental European companies are beginning to invest and grow. The USA and Japan are likely to be the first and second largest markets in the world for this company's products, and Germany is likely to be the third if we are looking to the future. Product planning, particularly new product planning in a company of this kind, must essentially become world-wide in its orientation and practice. This is easy to speak about and write about, but the recruitment of individuals with sufficient experience and breadth of thought and international understanding, who can build processes of global product planning, can be a very difficult business indeed.

Product planning is an essential and critical process within any company which seeks to grow through product enhancement and new product development over a period of time. Product planning in many British companies does not exist as a function at all. Product planning can be that function which receives inputs from customers, markets, sales groups, technologists, R & D departments, senior management and elsewhere, and distils those critical elements that pull together opportunity at the market end and capability at the technology and manufacturing end.

I recently enjoyed an extremely stimulating discussion with the director of research and development of a British public company which has been a world leader and is now in the process of fighting a growing number of international competitors. This company's products, while developed in a high-technology business centre in Britain, are essentially for world-wide consumption. The R & D director said to me: 'Please do all you can to convince my senior management that I can only run my research and development department effectively in terms of profitable new product development and turn out products which will have world-wide appeal *if* the board establishes an international marketing department or an international group of product planners who can help my people interface with marketing and sales groups and customers world-wide. We can really only develop well-defined new products if product planning is a well-developed function in our company.'

It is often the case in companies that while directors concern themselves with grand strategy and three-, five- or ten-year plans, attention is not paid to the building of a sufficiently adequate management infrastructure that takes care of important functions like product planning. In British Airways the chief executive at the time of writing, Sir Colin Marshall, is someone who becomes deeply involved in these kinds of issues. Just as he attends a very large number of seminars each year on subjects like 'Putting People First', he also spends a very considerable amount of time with help of BA experts sifting through the results of consumer research and proposals for product planning, proposals for product upgrade and enhancements which can lead BA (indeed have led it) to gain market share through genuine competitive advantage. In British Airways 'the product' can be ClubWorld or ClubEurope or First Class. I have travelled recently on BA and talked to cabin staff about the 'new product' which has been introduced both in Super Club and First Class. BA cabin staff have been extremely well informed about new products that have been introduced. Such products have obviously been the subject of excellent planning based on customer research and then field tests. Before they have been introduced to customers they have also been fully sold to the staff who eventually present them. Product planning is the function which designs new products, taking account of market needs and all of the technical scientific and other expertise in the company, crystallises a specification, conducts a reiterative process between functions such as R & D, marketing, production and quality, and eventually brings forth a distillation which can become a new product. The product-planning function in the best companies then sees this through by continuous involvement to the birth of a new product and has much to say about how that product shall be introduced to staff in the company, and customers.

Interesting questions for directors on this subject would relate to how much they know about what is going on in the company today relative to market and product development. Does the company employ a structured approach to marketing planning? Do we know what the marketing process is or how good it is? Does product planning as a concept and a practice exist in the company? Who is responsible for it? Do we know how it is being conducted? Investments in new product development, once commenced, have a habit of gathering momentum and being difficult to stop. This is not to suggest that is is not necessary in many industrial circumstances to allocate very large amounts of money to genuine research or new product development. Rather, it must be emphasised here, as it was at the beginning of this chapter, that there can be a very great yield in placing funds behind marketing and sales development of existing products and that directors should surely examine the potential in what is already available as an alternative to allocating large amounts of their own money or shareholders' funds to a speculative new product programme.

Two final sets of thoughts on product development. First, there is usually a need to develop the *process* whereby a product is made so as to maintain or improve quality; increase efficiency; and reduce cost. Process development may often be the province of manufacturing engineering but will inevitably involve R & D and quality staff, too. The impact of process change on the product and the development of new packaging methods will need the attention of product developers as well as process developers and, of course, cost will be involved. Second, innovation is not confined to devices, consumerable items, packaging or the production process. Innovative presentation, selling, distribution are other examples where positive change and competitive advantage may be sought and found. 'Marketing complete products' as espoused by Davidow (1986), is an approach favoured by many. It is also an approach with much to offer in exploiting new markets.

CHAPTER 7

———————— ,∾, ————————

EXPLORATION AND EXPLOITATION
– DIRECT AND INDIRECT APPROACHES

The directors of a company will decide on the precise approach to exploring and developing markets depending upon the size, maturity, situation and general condition of the particular organisation. Clearly a large multinational company is likely to have the resources to enable a good deal of market research to be done 'in house' and may also find it easy to make a decision to adopt a direct approach when it comes to implementing marketing and expansionist plans. However, some very large companies prefer to use cash to obtain the services of specialist marketing research organisations and business consultants because this can be more cost-effective, and also because they take the view that a totally independent and unbiased approach to a new opportunity, initiative or venture is preferable. There is, of course, a middle way where company resources join forces with outside help.

For the smaller company, paradoxically, although resources may be limited the only way quickly to gain certain market information may be by the use of purchased data or commissioned research. Similarly, the smaller, less mature company wishing to exploit overseas markets from the UK or regional markets from a central base may initially have no choice but the use of established distributors, agents, manufacturers' representatives or trading partners of one kind or another as a means of finding channels of distribution and getting its products sold.

In this chapter we consider some of the criteria which can be applied in deciding on direct, indirect, or mixed approaches.

EXPLORATION – WHAT DO WE KNOW AND WHAT CAN WE FIND OUT OURSELVES?

If we take the example of an established but still youthful company, with a turnover of, say, £10 million, operating in the medical laboratory diagnostic field and marketing a range of kits for carrying out diagnostic laboratory tests, it may well be that within the management group there exists a very great fund of knowledge about the fields of use for not only existing but also potential new products. Laboratory diagnostics is a highly focused business and it is likely that the principals of such a company and most of the management will have come from a medical laboratory or scientific background and some will have come from the diagnostic industry. Since in most countries sources of data on health care and the tracking of potential customers is relatively straightforward, a company in this kind of business may well decide to carry out its own exploration if it is in the process of moving into new geographical markets or if it is introducing a new range of products to expand its business in existing market sectors. Published data in this kind of business are often freely available, and the exploration can be carried out by those managers who will eventually recommend a decision and become responsible for implementation, so that continuity through the processes of market assessment, market entry, planning and execution may be assured. Of course, such a company may decide to buy a piece of very carefully focused market research using a specialist health-care research company or firm of consultants, and this investment may be more cost-effective than tying up operational management in the task. However, experience shows that unless operational management is close to consulting work and market research the effort can be either misdirected or diluted in such a way that the company fails to reap the full benefit of the work. The proper use of market research and consulting firms takes management time if it is to be fully successful.

Understanding trends in diagnostic medicine may take effort but finding the information is likely to be fairly easy. As a contrast, consider the overwhelming task facing a company like the Domino Group which, as already mentioned, markets high-technology product identification equipment into virtually every major industry to be found in the world today. Selling to health-care and pharmaceutical industries, cosmetics and toiletries, the dairy industry, the wire and cable industry, the lumber industry, the chemical industry, the electronics industry, the motor industries, the printing and addressing industries, and so on, makes it extraordinarily difficult for a company, especially a small or medium-sized one, to keep track of industry trends in one major country, let alone world-wide, especially when these trends are likely to be influenced by legislation and regulatory activity, environmental issues, health and safety at work – not to mention legislation on medicines affecting the way in which the pharmaceutical industry operates its manufacturing plants. Add to this the inexorable technological change which we see taking place in industry as a whole with the introduction of automation, robotics, computer science, and so on, and it is clear that the small to medium-sized company marketing industrial equipment industry-wide either takes its chances and sells by the seat of its pants, or conducts carefully structured research for each industry and explores current and future trends in ways which give direction relative to new geographical or industry sector opportunities, and also points the way to new product planning and product development to give some likelihood of competitive advantage, market-share growth, and the attainment or maintenance of leadership. For an industrial company of this kind, once it is past the newborn stage, the use of specialist sources for market exploration is inevitable.

Directors of the smaller company may find that exploration of new market opportunities works best if it is structured in a way which enables the researcher, whether he or she is a company employee or an outside agent, to take simple questions and concepts to respondents and to get clear answers which provide direction or help set priorities in deciding where to go for market development rather than to conduct voluminous open-ended statistical market research. We can return to a larger company, British Airways, by way of example. When interviewing travellers, British Airways does not ask a series of open-ended questions such as 'What kind of seat would you find most comfortable?' or 'What routes would you like to see opened up?' It takes to respondents a concept: 'Please come and try out this new airline seat which we are thinking of introducing to our transatlantic routes. Please try out the controls in the following way . . . Now, please respond to the questions I will ask you. Please comment on the visual and sound quality of this small individual video I am about to show you . . . .' The results of testing concepts like this may be the evolution of a new or enhanced product, or the emergence of new questions and new ideas or pursuit of market development. In the same way the industrial company which we referred to earlier in the chapter, after having obtained some basic data about the structure of industry in a new country, might get answers to its questions about the likely success of market entry with a certain product by going there, perhaps with some local assistance, and demonstrating the product to a range of industrialists and getting some clear answers to structured questions about the concept being shown. If indirect resources are to be used for this kind of exploration, there will be a requirement for the commissioning company to train the outside agents very carefully. In a technology business it is more likely that direct company resources will require to be involved in such an exploration. In consumer fields it is hard to envisage how exploration of new markets, either geographical, consumer-group or product-related, can be adequately researched prior to a new market investment without substantial structured work carried out by skilled in-house or independent workers.

EXPLOITATION – HOW DO WE REACH THE MARKET?

For the large established company this question is likely to be posed only when entering markets with a new product or moving into entirely new parts of the world (which is quite unusual with very large companies, which tend to be multinational). For the fast-growing small and medium-sized company which may have established a good solid base in the home country, once it is known that world markets exist for the product and once there has been some prioritisation of target territories, a significant question arises as to whether it is going to be more appropriate to establish subsidiary companies or deal through third-party distributors. As we have already stated, the smaller newer company will almost inevitably be forced to go through third-party distributors by virtue of resource constraints. The company with a strong home base which has ample cash or access to funds may well have a choice, however. This is a good point at which to look at the pros and cons of direct versus indirect approaches to the development of international markets.

Table 7.1 shows some of the pros and cons which need to be considered in making the direct versus indirect decision. The list is by no means complete and the question admits of no easy answer.

It is essentially a question of 'horses for courses'. There is no point in deciding on the distributor route if no suitable distributor candidates are known to exist in the country in question. Before conducting an elaborate enquiry into the

Table 7.1 Approaches to the development of new foreign markets

Direct (subsidiary operations)	Indirect (independent distributor or agent)
● Significant start-up costs	● Little or no start-up costs
● Working capital commitments may be considerable	● No direct working capital commitment
● Possible exposure on receivables and bad debts	● Distributor bears the receivables exposure
● Direct control over selling and market resources	● Low level of control or no control over actions of distributor staff
● Flexibility to 'beef up' investment and resourcing if opportunity indicates the wisdom of this	● May be very difficult to get distributor to invest resources of quality and quantity
● Control over quality of technical resources and support in an industrial business	● Limited control over quality and quantity of technical resources supporting distributor business

best route to take, it is worth doing some fast and simple research to discover what kind of trading partners *do* exist. There are various services available to assist in this task. The Department of Trade and Industry, through various offices of overseas trade, can be very helpful, and independent consultants are also available with specialist knowledge of various markets.

Our considerations here have focused largely on finding channels for marketing and distribution in new markets. For the large established company with manufacturing facilities world-wide the decision pathway may be different and could be virtually automatic if a network of international wholly-owned subsidiaries exists. For the small or medium-sized industrial company with products manufactured by contracted third parties or a single manufacturing operation based in a single country, decisions on how to exploit international markets through direct or indirect means are likely to be crucial. Some companies take the view that a direct presence in the world's most important markets is preferable to provide a core of enduring business units, all or some of which can appoint distributors and export to various parts of the world. Other young companies have found that, having started with the distribution route, it has become necessary to establish a presence in certain key countries in Europe or in North America. Starting a direct business in Japan is much more difficult and many companies have tended to take the distributor route or to find a means to establish a joint venture with a Japanese company. Although such ventures can work well, the cost involved is unlikely to be justified or bearable until a significant level of business can be predicted. Many UK companies now operating joint ventures in Japan began by selecting a distributor or trading partner, building a business and evolving the joint venture from that point.

We go on in the next two chapters to consider in more detail how to find, select, train and manage distributor business partners. There is neither time nor space in this volume to discuss in detail the establishment of overseas subsidiaries (this is a subject in itself), but such a decision should be taken with great care and the close involvement of directors. The route of using distributors can only be followed if it is known that suitable candidate companies exist in the geographical or sectorial markets to be attacked. The absence of such companies may well assist company directors in prioritising where to go first or sometimes where not to go at all.

Whether the direct or indirect approach is taken, comments made earlier in the book about the need to prioritise new market opportunities should be borne in mind, since even if the exploration has been done and large market opportunities identified in a variety of countries, a small or medium-sized organisation will only be able to appoint, train, establish and push forward a certain number of new major distribution channels at any point in time.

CHAPTER 8

— ☙ —

DISTRIBUTORS, DEALERS AND TRADING PARTNERS – PRACTICAL CONSIDERATIONS AND APPROACHES

TYPES OF BUSINESS PARTNER

Having made the decision to enter a particular territory or industry segment with the help of a third party, the next step is to decide which type of distributor or agent is likely to be best for a specific business.

Let us take the example of a UK-based company manufacturing a 'mid-technology' piece of equipment used widely in the packaging industry. This company produces products which require particular attention in respect of specification, selection, installation, after-sales service and the supply of compatible consumable products. If we assume that the company is a fully integrated sales and service company in the UK with its own team of technical support personnel, then the choices which face it as it embarks on a plan to enter the French market through a third-party trading partner would include:

- A full service distributor. Having agreed a price to pay the UK company which would include a suitable discount on the expected end-user price, this partner would import, stock and sell products and commit himself to customer training and to having on his staff trained technical people to install and service equipment. He would also be committing himself to completing customer service, including the stocking and supply of consumables.
- Selling and stocking distributor. This trading partner would employ a salesforce and would import and sell the products of the UK company, would stock equipment and spare parts, and even consumables, but would provide no technical support. The UK company in this case would need to provide such support out of the UK (a difficult and potentially dangerous decision to take), or to find a contract technical service company in France and to provide adequate training to the staff of this company who would perform the service independently of the

72

selling and stocking distributor or as a sub-contractor to the primary distributor in France.

- Selling agent. A selling agent in France would simply, either himself or through his staff, obtain orders for the product of the UK company and submit these to the UK. The UK company would then take full responsibility for the specification, the quotation, the sale itself, exportation from the UK, importation into France and delivery to the customer. Either directly or through a contract technical service company, as described in the last example, the UK company would assume full responsibility for installation and for after-sales service and the supply of consumables. The selling agent would receive a straightforward commission on the sale.

We can see already that without elaborating the detail, there are a number of variations on the theme of distribution. We will in a moment examine the thought process which needs to be undertaken before deciding on the most suitable approach for directors of a company to take. Let us continue with two more options which could be available to our UK industrial company wishing to penetrate the French market.

- Manufacturer's representative. The difference between a manufacturer's representative and an agent may in some instances be slight. The manufacturers' representative is likely to be a salesman operating in the field selling a range of products. He will simply take orders or even pass on leads to the company in question or to a full service or selling distributor or an established agent who may have administrative resources which the field-based individual may lack. Manufacturer's representatives are generally appointed for a defined geographical area either by distributors or by the principal company producing the product.
- Original equipment manufacturer (OEM). This terminology is becoming increasingly used in industrial circles and refers to a company which is likely to be a producer of an integrated production system. For instance, dairy-industry companies such as the Swedish organisation Tetra-Pak, are designers, builders and suppliers of large-scale integrated equipment for fabricating and filling the waxed cardboard cartons into which our milk is packaged. The Tetra-Pak company is an extremely interesting company which is one of the largest paper converters in Europe. Tetra-Pak's *real* business is the production of the material from which the milk and fruit juice containers are produced. The elaborate filling equipment which it provides on rental (not usually for sale) is the razor which takes ever increasing numbers of blades, which in this case are milk cartons! From time to time companies like Tetra-Pak will wish to integrate into the

normal production line an additional piece of packaging equipment, for example a specialist unit for printing variable information such as the expiry date on the carton. In some instances Tetra-Pak will purchase the unit and sell it on with the whole of the large-scale filling system. In many production processes where a company like Tetra-Pak or a project management company pulls together a range of equipment for a factory requiring machinery for an integrated manufacturing process, the project management company will become the 'OEM' and will buy units from other manufacturing companies and take responsibility for the marketing, installation and the training and support of staff of the purchaser. In other instances OEMs will simply buy, integrate and ship and the supplier of the industrial unit or his appointed distributor in a particular territory will pick up the ongoing responsibility for technical support and consumables supplied.

Although it has not been dealt with in detail in this book, the process of finding trading partners or associates for companies working in the service industries is equally important. Accounting firms, for instance – apart from the biggest firms who tend to have offices world-wide, who work with clients based in one country but who have international businesses – will often find the need to operate with recommended 'associates' in different parts of the world. This assists clients of the accounting company to achieve coherence and continuity in their overall operation, and enables them to relate to one operation for consolidation processes in their home country. By finding associates to help one important client, small and medium-sized accounting firms can find that their business thus expands internationally. They may have a particular product which they can then promote through an international network. The criteria which would need to be applied by the principals and directors of an accounting company expanding in this way into new markets would need to be as comprehensive as those discussed in this chapter for industrial and consumer companies. A unique service is provided to multinational companies who wish to move staff around frequently, which entails the commissioning of a newly formed company handling international removal and relocation work for the managers and employees being transferred or seconded. This international removal business is essentially a consortium of removal firms who have agreed to work together and to fund the means for central co-ordination and administration. This is an interesting example of a service industry focusing on an obvious market opportunity and finding trading partners so as to offer a unique world-wide service to global clients.

We have identified a number of approaches which our UK-based supplier of industrial equipment may consider taking when entering the French market. The selection does not in all cases need to be an exclusive one. Full service distributors can work with OEMs and also sometimes employ selling agents.

DECIDING ON THE MOST APPROPRIATE TYPE OF DISTRIBUTORS

What are the decision criteria which directors need to apply in coming to a decision on the type of distribution which is likely to be most appropriate? The following would be of primary importance:

- The financial position of the company. Selling through a full service distributor will cost more in terms of the discount they will take than selling through an agent or an OEM. The company's business and financial planning will dictate in some measure the kind of trading partner considered most suitable.

- Competitive positioning and presence. If the UK company is to succeed in penetrating a market in France and building up a useful business and if competition, perhaps local competition, is strong with a full sales and service operation in place, the only way to obtain a substantial piece of business may be to work through a distributor willing to invest in full service resources. The full service distributor will need to employ significant resources and will carry a substantial overhead. In most instances he will be handling a range of products but in some circumstances may be established solely to handle the UK company's products. If the latter is the case (and it is most unusual) then he may demand an even larger discount on the end-user selling price because his overheads will only be recovered through the one product line.

- Although many industrial companies use the exhibition vehicle to gain awareness of and interest in their products and open leads, they still need to follow through with demonstrations, customer training, installation and full after-sales service support. Some products are simply unsaleable without the employment of properly trained salespeople or sales engineers who, supported by extensive exhibition and promotional work, call on the customer to demonstrate the product, make the proposal for a specified installation and take the order, subsequently providing follow-up services. If direct sales are a critical issue for a company in gaining business, then adequate coverage of a territory such as the French example we have taken will be a major consideration. In many instances, directors will feel inclined to go for a relationship with a full service distributor who will hire and train sales people, ensure that the country is well covered, manage the salesmen in the field and provide all the administrative support that salesforces need. Managing a business out of the UK through a fragmented collection of selling agents and manufacturers' representatives in France may be difficult, although here again UK companies do sometimes operate in this way, employing a support organisation in Britain which informs, monitors, and follows up the work of independent agents or manufacturer's representative in an overseas territory.

- The technical content of the product will be a major consideration. If a product is complex and requires customisation, as is the case with many types of industrial equipment, then any company exporting out of the UK will need to provide adequate technical resource in the territory to be exploited, not only to get the product sold but also to enjoy continued support of demanding industrial customers who will require ongoing attention and technical service. Here again, many industrial UK and US companies using third parties for export sales will go for those who have technical resources or are prepared to hire and train the right kinds of people. Even in these cases the amount of planning and work and continuous follow-up required in the home country to support these distributors must not be underestimated. Because a company appoints a full service distributor in France does not mean that few or no resources will be required in the UK in support of this business. This issue is discussed in more detail in the next chapter.

- The type of service requirement must also be considered when deciding on a particular type of distribution in an overseas country, or in any territory or in a region of the UK or the USA. Some businesses require intimate attention to detail day by day in service and customer contacts. Obviously, when exploiting an overseas market for this kind of business, there will be a requirement for access to appropriate qualified knowledgeable staff for customers who can speak to the supplying company in its own language. This type of business is likely to require a full service distributor partner.

All of this discussion largely relates to manufacturing/marketing companies offering equipment or technological goods to industry. For some companies in other industries the decisions on which channels of distribution and which type of distributor to use may be much simpler. For instance, many countries have established channels of distribution for pharmaceutical and health-care products. The regulatory mechanisms in particular countries may simply dictate those channels which are available and the chain of supply from producer to customer may be so well established as to provide no alternative. For instance, in the United Kingdom itself a company entering the pharmaceutical business, be it as a producer or as a distributing subsidiary of an overseas company, will find the only means to get prescription medicines used and available when doctors prescribe them and hand the prescription to the patient, is to put those products into the chain of supply which works its way through pharmaceutical wholesaler, retail pharmacy or hospital dispensary and hence to the eventual consumer. Not only is this structure of distribution established physically, but all parts of the chain are licensed and controlled by legislation on medicines. Therefore if our UK company were in the pharmaceutical business and planned to export to France, apart from the time which might be taken to get the preparation registered under French medicines law, there would be a clear structure of distribution which would be unavoidable.

In the consumer products field, one can see that only companies with substantial resources will be in a position to market and promote to consumers in any territory, although this can be done through third parties and it would not be unusual to find a consumer company based in the UK organising its direct promotion through advertising and public relations agencies and overseas territory, and distributing its products through a recognised wholesale to retail chain. The type of distribution available to get retail products on the shelf where the consumer can buy them is not so varied as we have discussed in industrial marketing.

FINDING DISTRIBUTION CANDIDATES

Let us again assume we are directors of a UK-based industrial company which manufactures a piece of equipment which has found favour in the UK. We have decided that this equipment needs to be sold in overseas territories through third-party full service distributors. We have decided on the countries we wish to attack in sequence and we are now, with no previous experience of such activity, beginning to seek specific candidates as trading partners. Where are the sources of information? (While I have taken a UK example, the comments which follow could apply to any EEC country, to Scandinavia or to North America, where equivalent sources of information will be found.) Here are some of the most likely:

- Internal records and reports (there may have been visits to territories in the past). It is always worth looking in-house first.
- The Department of Trade and Industry and British Overseas Trade Board. Excellent services exist both centrally and regionally and a wealth of information can be provided from DTI sources. Local or regional DTI

staff can be visited and will also visit companies. Services are structured so as to provide specific information from knowledgeable sources about specific geographical areas especially relative to exports. The DTI, as previously stated, is a good source of information about overseas markets, for its reference lists of distributors and possible companies to work with, overseas as well as in the UK. It should be an early port of call.

- Libraries, both general libraries and business libraries, are an excellent source of data not only on overseas and industry-based markets but also of companies working as distributors and agents within them. From libraries as well as the DTI, central sources of information in particular countries can also be found. There will always be in overseas countries some government-supported agency able to connect with UK companies which need to do business.

- Banks, including merchant banks. Both in the UK and particularly in overseas territories banks, especially merchant banks, can be excellent door-openers on sources of information for the finding of trading partners and introductions to specific companies.

- Trade directories. A multitude exist and cover the world. Much information on available distributors can be uncovered.

- Industry associations. Again, both in the UK and in overseas territories, most identifiable industries are organised in associations. In some industries there are a number of trade associations. In many industries there are associations devoted to distribution companies. Access to these associations is not difficult since their members are naturally anxious to continue business growth and to make contact with those likely to bring future profitable growth.

- Exhibitions and trade shows. Especially in the industrial field exhibitions and trade shows are an extremely important part of the awareness-creating and selling processes. Many exhibitors are distributors and at all trade shows and exhibitions those looking for companies and products to represent will be found. Therefore, a UK company seeking overseas distribution which takes a stand at an exhibition may find that a great deal of attention is given by local people who feel they may be potential distributors. Additionally, those running or managing distribution companies will travel the world and attend all the major exhibitions in search of new product lines.

- Agencies and consultants. When exploring overseas territories and looking for distributors, an effective route to the right people and a degree of preparation in approaching them and obtaining reports and information can be through the use of specialist agencies and consultants. This will require an initial outlay which could be substantial but may prove to be the most effective route in the long run if the consultant is truly knowledgeable about the market to be exploited and particularly if he and his staff have contacts and language ability.

RESEARCH AND PREPARATION FOR THE SELECTION OF DISTRIBUTORS

We have just discussed an example of the value of research and preparation leading up to the selection process. The involvement of the chairman and/or chief executive and certainly directors in the process leading up to the final selection and appointment of trading partners is strongly recommended. Indeed, this is not simply a one-way process – the distributor is also considering whether or not to take on the supplier. The trading partner being considered may be a company of repute whose managers have many years of success behind them and have built up a prominent position in the market. Such a trading partner may be willing to enter into serious discussions about working for a supplying company only if these discussions ultimately take place at an appropriately high level.

In order that the right people can be involved in the selection process and make the most efficient use of valuable management time, research and preparation in advance of meeting with distributor candidates are an essential investment. Having armed yourself with relevant information on the country in which your potential distributors are based – its size; current situation; regulatory, market and industry trends; and the state of competition – you will then need a report, prepared either by your own staff or by outside consultants, on those candidates who have got past the first screening procedures of financial viability and suitability. Ideally, it should cover the following matters of interest:

- Size and growth and financial factors and assessment
- Activities: products and markets
- Management and organisation
- Assessment of sales and technical ability, including information on the sales and technical workforces
- Assessment of the company by business people of the principals of other distributors known to you in the same country
- Assessment of known customers of this distributor relative to reputation, service and reliability
- The distributor's facilities – report on site visits
- The distributor's willingness to invest in training; management time; sales and promotion; support resources; and inventory.

EXCHANGE VISITS

In the industrial field it is a golden rule that no distributor is appointed without a visit to his premises from a member of a senior management team of the company wishing to make the appointment. The chairman or chief executive should definitely visit full-line distributors and meet the owners or directors of the distributor business. This is not simply to visit facilities and check over physical things. In industrial marketing the quality of relationship between managements of supplying companies and distributors is a critical issue. I use the term 'trading partner' advisedly. A balanced relationship between principal and distributor is crucial and there needs to be, for optimal effectiveness, a joint approach to business strategy and to business planning. The distributor owners or managers must be sympathetic to the business aims of the supplying company. Even if there is a willingness to invest, some matching of cultures to a degree is essential. A clear understanding between the most senior managers in each organisation that there is to be forward momentum based on joint plans and commitments, and trust and confidence between senior executives on each side, are more important even than the written agreements which will eventually have to be drawn up (these are discussed later in this chapter).

Before final selection of distributors, the chief executive or a suitably qualified company director should visit the distributor owners or managers for substantial final discussions and a review of facilities. The distributor management should also visit the supplying company's headquarters and main production area. Indeed, suspicions should be aroused as to the thoroughness and business sense of distributors who would be prepared to accept a distributorship without visiting the supplier's premises and meeting the key people on the team. There are many things in business life which can and should be delegated, but decisions on placing business in the hands of third parties in overseas countries are not among the decisions a chief executive should ever delegate entirely.

FINAL DECISIONS AND APPOINTMENTS

A good process for a company to follow is for the chief executive, the marketing director or other executives concerned with the particular overseas market or business sector, once all the visits are done, to confer with sufficient time available and to draw up appropriate lists of pros and cons of candidate companies visited (assuming there has been more than one). The final selection can then be made and the first-choice candidate notified and offered outline terms and conditions. It is always a good thing, if there are second and third choices, to keep them 'on ice' while the first approaches are made because it is not always the case that offers are accepted. The final decision should not be made known to a distributor candidate at the end of a first visit even though the decision may have been made mentally in the presence of an outstanding company. It is always a good thing to give time for consideration and thinking through and to maintain attention in the relationship through the last stages of decision-making. This will often bring about revelations which otherwise may not have been made, or may cause initiatives to be taken by the distributor to commit more than he would otherwise do by way of resources if he feels he is unlikely otherwise to get the decision. The final agreement to appoint should be ratified as soon after the decision is made as possible.

AGREEMENTS, CONTRACTS, TERMS AND CONDITIONS

Figure 8.1 gives the kind of 'small print' terms and conditions which most companies publish on the back of written quotations. When appointing third-party trading partners a written contract or agreement is necessary, although, as previously stated, more important than the paper are the trust, the confidence and the intent which exist between the parties.

CONDITIONS OF ORDER

1.   The company placing the Order on the front of this form is hereinafter called "the Purchaser" and the person, firm or company to whom the Order on the front of this form is addressed is hereinafter called "the Seller".

2.   Any objection to these conditions must be raised and settled before the order is accepted.

3.   In the event of the seller being unable to comply with the delivery instructions in this order the seller must inform the purchaser of this fact. The purchaser will be at liberty to vary the terms of this order or cancel the same as the purchaser thinks fit and will notify the seller of any such variation or cancellation.

4.   Whenever in this order delivery is requested within a fixed time, such time shall be of the essence of the contract and if the seller does not deliver the goods ordered within the time stated the purchaser may treat such non-delivery as a breach of the conditions of the contract which will give the purchaser the right to reject the goods and treat the contract as repudiated and recover damages from the seller for any loss sustained by the purchaser by reason of such breach.
      Provided, however, that in the event that the seller suffers delay in performance due to an act of God or of the public enemy, military authority, fire, flood, strike, riot or sabotage, the time of completion shall be extended by a period of time equal to the period of such delay if the seller gives the purchaser notice in writing of the cause of any such delay within a reasonable time after the beginning thereof.

5.   Notwithstanding the conditions herein contained the purchaser may as and when it thinks fit vary the time of the delivery of the goods ordered but for such time as varied shall nevertheless be of the essence of the contract and special condition (3) hereof shall apply to such time as varied.

6.   The goods supplied under this order shall conform to the specifications laid down by the purchaser and be made of the best materials and to the entire satisfaction of the purchaser. In the event of a breach of this condition the purchaser shall be entitled:
      (a)   to reject either all the goods ordered by this order or such part of them as it is dissatisfied with and/or
      (b)   to claim damages for any loss sustained by it by reason of such rejection and/or
      (c)   to treat the contract as repudiated.

7. If goods are delivered in excess of quantity ordered and/or in excess of the delivery schedule placed on the seller then the purchaser may reject the excess quantity of such goods and return them to the seller at the seller's expense.

8. No responsibility is accepted for non-receipt of goods despatched.

9. Save as to goods herein specified, consisting of materials and articles of standard design and not made to the purchaser's specification, the seller agrees that during the period of execution of this order and for a further period of two years thereafter he/they will not manufacture or procure to be manufactured by any other person, firm or company any of the goods substantially similar thereto or disclose to any person, firm or company any manufacturing process or trade secret or other information whatsoever relating to the said goods.

10. The purchaser's messengers are authorised to collect goods intended for the purchaser and to sign for them "unexamined" but not otherwise and the purchaser reserves the right to reject such goods in whole or in part upon examination at the specified destination within a reasonable time of delivery.

11. If the business of the purchaser shall be stopped, interrupted or restricted by riot, lockout, strike (whether of the employees of the purchaser or of any other persons), fire, explosion or any other cause whatsoever the purchaser shall have the right to cancel this order in respect of any goods undelivered at the date of such cancellation by informing the seller by any method and/or to defer the date of delivery and of payment until the business of the purchaser shall be re-opened.

12. The seller will indemnify the purchaser against all action costs claims, damages, demands and liabilities for or in respect of any proceedings brought or threatened to be brought against either the purchaser or its customers or any of them by any person being a patentee or other person alleging that the goods ordered or the sale thereof by it or its customers constitutes an infringement of a patent or a passing-off.

13. All tools, gauges, dies, jigs, fixtures or patterns, which the seller specially makes or requires for the manufacture of goods specified in this order shall be used for the manufacture of such goods exclusively to the order of the purchaser and not for any other purpose or for any other customer. The seller agrees to keep such special tools, gauges, dies, jigs, fixtures and patterns in good order and repair and where these are not already the sole property of the purchaser, grants to the purchaser the option to acquire the same, or any one or more of them, on payment of the written-down value thereof as appearing in the seller's books at the date of exercise of the option credit being given for any payment made by the purchaser towards the original cost of purchase or manufacture.

14. In all orders placed with contracts which provide for payment on account, all materials, equipment, fittings, articles or things which the contractors shall acquire or allocate for incorporation in the work to be carried out under the order shall, without prejudice to the right of the purchaser of rejection, forthwith vest in and be the absolute property of the purchaser free from any lieu of unpaid purchase money, or otherwise.

15. All packing charges imposed by the seller (if any) must be notified to the purchaser separately.

16. A packing note describing the goods sold and the cases in which they or each of them are packed must accompany each and every delivery.

17. All returnable reels and containers must bear the seller's full name and address failing which the purchaser will be under no liability to pay for or in respect of them.

18. Nothing in these conditions shall prejudice any condition or warranty (express or implied) or other right or remedy to which the purchaser is entitled in relation to the said goods or work the subject of this order by virtue of any statute or custom or the general law or any local law or regulation.

19. This order is placed on the understanding that the property in any material supplied by the purchaser to the seller in connection with this order shall not be vested in the seller, but shall nevertheless be insured by the seller at the seller's own expense against fire (but not war risks) at its primary value plus any increased value that may arise in consequence of the seller having worked upon it.

20. No increase in the price quoted on this order will be effective unless and until approved in writing by the purchaser.

21. This order is placed with the seller by the purchaser on the express condition that if accepted by the seller it will be deemed to have been accepted by the seller on the express condition that no information of any kind whatsoever regarding this order, whether as to the nature, quantity or quality of the goods or materials hereby ordered or otherwise howsoever shall be divulged or disclosed by the seller or any of the seller's servants or agents to any person or persons (including any body corporate or incorporate) whomsoever, without the prior written consent of the purchaser.

22. This order must not be sub-contracted without the purchaser's permission.

23. Should any item being supplied to this order be of foreign origin the country of origin must be clearly indicated on all acknowledgements and invoices. When goods originate from the U.S.A. any ultimate destination clauses and endorsements on the original invoices or U.S. Shipping Documents must be made known to us.

Figure 8.1   Typical terms and conditions of purchase and sale.

The writing of agreements involves lawyers, who tend to be extremely cautious people (that's what we pay them for!), and it can become a laborious affair. An appropriate agreement should cover issues such as:

- Period of agreement
- Territory
- Fields of use
- Exclusivity (where applicable)
- Volume of sales to be met
- Prices and discounts
- Payment and credit terms
- Price revision procedures
- Review and performance appraisal
- Termination.

A copy of the kind of agreement used with success by many industrial companies is included in the appendix to this book.

With regard to periods of agreement, a useful approach is to operate with an initial trial period of one year, although most distributors wish for at least two, citing the very realistic argument that it takes time to get established and the fruits of labour do not flow through until the second and often the third year of activity, whereas investment all goes in 'up front'. Therefore an agreement which recognises a two- or three-year term, but allows termination earlier if certain conditions are not met, can be useful.

It is essential to include volume targets as part of the set of conditions under which the agreement is to be renewed or remain exclusive. Directors not experienced in working with such agreements should beware of the issue of exclusivity. Exclusivity is certainly a valid demand from a distributor who is going to invest significantly in building an organisation and a business in a particular country. But exclusivity unrelated to a committed volume of sales is a one-way track. A company can find itself locked out of a market for a number of years if a distributor has an exclusive contract unrelated to performance. The example of the agreement given in the appendix shows how this issue can be dealt with. Exclusivity ceases to be the right of the distributor if certain performance factors are not met. Loss of exclusivity often precedes termination in agreements with distributors.

Agreements should be reviewed at least annually and it is important that they be drawn up with proper legal advice. It is a truism that if agreements have to be enforced through the courts then essentially they have failed as business agreements and the relationship between the parties will clearly have failed. However, in some countries in the world, most particularly the USA, litigation and the involvement of lawyers in many aspects of business life is an expensive reality, and when signing agreements directors should be very clear that they are accepting legal obligations and that in some instances the agreement will be used or misused by the principals of another company for financial or business gain. The chief executive, chairman, or director responsible for any business must take the time to understand the agreements which are being signed on behalf of the company with third parties if not signing them himself or herself. At the end of the day he or she will be the responsible party and will be answerable to shareholders, if the company is public, if legal battles and resultant heavy expenses ensue from disputes regarding such agreements.

Some companies prefer to run without written agreements. This can work, especially if the relationships between people are particularly strong. However, at times of organisational change, the acquisition or merger of businesses, it is the written agreements which will protect one or both parties. Therefore, reiterating the principle of trust and confidence and joint planning being the real basis of successful business relationships, it must be said that the written agreement is essentially a necessary evil.

MANAGEMENT SUPPORT AND MEASUREMENT OF DISTRIBUTOR RELATIONSHIPS

As directors of a UK company, we have now gone through the decision process of naming the full-line distributor route as the one we need to take in France, we have found candidates, we have been through the process of joint visits, and we have selected an outstanding company based centrally in France to be our third-party distributor in that country for a range of industrial products. Is that the end of the story? Far from it! It is true to say that many distributors fail and are cursed by the companies that appoint them, largely because of a lack of direction, training and support. Those companies which work most effectively with distributors, having selected groups who are culturally compatible (from a business culture perspective) with the principal company, have invested very significantly in programmes of direction, training, support and management of distributor staff.

So having appointed our distributor, what are the next steps we must undertake in order to get him and his people moving and our business established? Before outlining those steps, there is an absolute principle for running successful distributor businesses:

Have an appropriate distributor support organisation management and structure.

For the company starting off with overseas distribution, there will be a requirement to have one home-based manager responsible for the distributor business. This may well be an export manager. If a number of distributors are appointed rapidly there will be a need to establish a sales desk through which their calls can pass and full-time or nominated part-time individuals in the organisation will need to be allocated to deal with administrative questions, technical questions, product enquiries, and so on. Clear announcements on the appointment of distributors and the names of those who will be calling in should be properly disseminated throughout the UK principal's organisation. Switchboard staff should be trained so as to be able to handle a new kind of activity – calls coming in from overseas – and should be clearly informed how to deal with these calls and where to route them. At the beginning of this book I spoke of a company-wide approach to quality improvement. Quality for the customer (and a distributor is an intermediary customer) begins with the first words that are spoken during a telephone conversation. The issue of culture and linguistics needs to be addressed by companies entering into an international business. A complete section in Chapter 9 is included on aspects of training and staff attitudes to international business and overseas customers and trading partners.

Figure 8.2 shows a model for the sales department of a company well established in home and export business. Many industrial companies marketing equipment world-wide organise themselves in this way. The sales managers responsible for regional activities in Europe and the Americas are based in the UK in this example, but travel extensively. They are backed

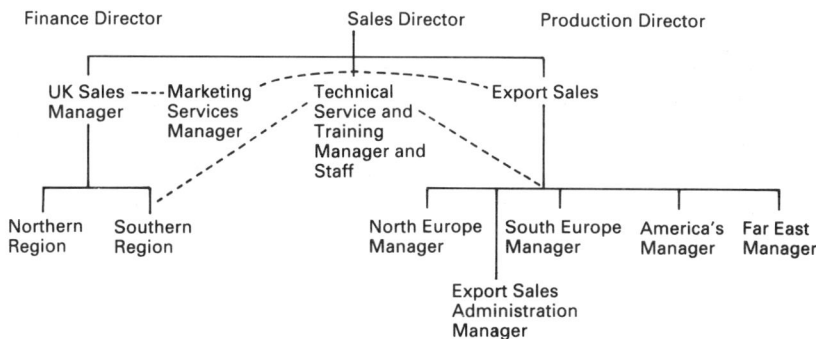

Figure 8.2 Sales organisations for a UK and international industrial business.

up by a strong administration group, which handles orders and enquiries, and share the services of technical service and training and marketing service groups.

Let us assume that, either as a new exploiter of overseas markets, we have our small group in place, or, as an established company with an international network having just appointed a new distributor, we are ready to go. We might even be appointing a dealer to handle our business in another part of our home territory. The principles will be the same, and the steps which will need to be followed will include:

1. Training distributor and staff:
   - Market and industry applications training
   - Technical and 'hands-on' training
   - Sales training
   - Our company and 'the way we do things'
   - Company products: (i) features and benefits
     (ii) sales arguments
   - Competitors and competitive products
   - Selling against competition.
2. Establishing a joint understanding of the market opportunity:
   - Development of a business plan and a sales forecast
   - Programme of visits, follow-up training and review meetings
   - Joint promotional programme.

One of the particular challenges in establishing appropriate relationships with distributors is, while having a good strong rapport between people, to be able to stand back and review results objectively, as is necessary in any business enterprise. Dealing with underperformance is essential: with all the best intentions, the best search and selection procedures, the thorough training and preparation which have been discussed, it is still a reality of business life that sometimes *things go wrong*.

An interesting case from the field of industrial marketing is that of a Japanese company which was given by a British company a wide-ranging agreement to market its products in Japan and virtually the whole of the Far East. The Japanese company had its main base in Japan, and as most international business people will know, for a variety of reasons, historical and cultural, it is often difficult for Japanese business people to gain acceptance in some of the countries inhabited mostly by Chinese and other ethnic groups. In view of this, the Japanese distributor allocated resources to travel around various of the territories, including Hong Kong, Singapore, Korea, and thus spreading the company's talents to the point where the Japanese business was not growing at a rate in line with minimum targets agreed in the original contract. The Japanese company was anxious to retain all of the territories and defended its position on the basis that it was competing with an enormous Japanese company in Japan which was preventing market share growth. A review meeting took place between a relatively new chief executive of the principal company and the Japanese distributor management, and in the most polite way it was made clear that the agreement would be enforced and that the results in Japan were unacceptable. The Japanese company was urged to focus sufficient resources on growing the Japanese market (the second largest in the world for the products in question) and since no measurable sales had been made in the remaining territories the principal company did not give the Japanese distributor time to perform and retain exclusivity, but in certain countries initiated a 'two-horse race' for a period of time enabling other distributors to sell non-exclusively.

The outcome in this particular case was an extremely happy one for all parties. The Japanese company, by investing proper resources in the Japanese business, where the prices enjoyed are still the highest in the world, expanded its business and its profitability substantially. Other companies invited to participate in some of the smaller countries of the Far East got off to a flying start, and by their local presence and enthusiasm quickly established a very significant business for the principal company. The clarity and firmness of the executive group of the principals and the way in which the negotiations were handled, with appropriate tact, diplomacy and acknowledgement of cultural differences, were key factors in bringing out, over a period of two years, a positive set of outcomes from a difficult situation. Indeed the positive outcomes are continuing for all concerned today. The point about this case is that once again the involvement of the most senior executives in the company at a time of tense negotiations and difficult decisions was a critical factor in finding a positive way forward.

A process of regular review meetings with distributor management is an essential way of dealing with underperformance and, indeed, many other aspects of relationships with the distributors. It is essential that underperformance be recognised, acknowledged, and dealt with firmly, and again I emphasise the importance of senior management in ensuring that the principle is adhered to throughout an organisation.

The ultimate action in dealing with persistent underperformance is the termination of a relationship. This can be difficult and costly, especially if the relationship has lasted a number of years and for some reason suddenly goes wrong. If both sides have committed themselves to an appropriate agreement, the issue of termination should become straightforward in the event that it is necessary. It is not a step which should be put off once it has been seen to be inevitable. It should also involve senior members of the management team to ensure that it is done with appropriate consideration of business ethics and also to make certain that the company does not become liable to legal action and find itself in a long drawn-out expensive wrangle with a disillusioned distributor.

Discussion in this chapter has been taken to some level of detail because it is among the most important in the book. The large majority of young and growing UK, European and US-based companies seeking to exploit overseas markets or new industry sectors will be working with trading partners. Typically it will take one-and-a-half to two years to get a new distributor up and running, so mistakes can be very costly in terms of profit and time. Attention to detail is essential.

CHAPTER 9

—— ·❧· ——

ORGANISING PLANNING AND
RESOURCING FOR
NEW MARKET INITIATIVES

Previous chapters of this book have already touched on aspects of organising to support new market initiatives. So important are some of the activities needed to give a good chance of success that they are discussed in more detail in this chapter.

COMMITTING SKILLED RESOURCES

Even the smallest company of three or four people will achieve greater success if individuals are experienced and practised in aspects of marketing and if there is a suitable concentration of energy into definable goals. Focus is important and the experience and skill, the will and determination exhibited by groups or individuals in large or small companies will ultimately determine the degree of success. Attitude is an important aspect of human resources aiming to take new initiatives in new industry sectors or in new countries. The role of directors and especially the chief executive in clarifying goals and building organisations with clear objectives is a critical one in companies of all sizes seeking to enter new markets. A new market initiative is likely to fail if an already busy or possibly overwhelmed manager or group is thrown a new project to 'add on' to existing items. The chief executive personally needs to have the ability and experience to think though the implications of deciding on new market initiatives, and of organisational structure. Management structure and process also need to be built into any new activity in an industry sector or an export market. Directors must determine how many new country or sectorial markets can be tackled at any time or over a defined period. Simply adding people is *not* usually a satisfactory way to handle more market initiatives suddenly, although competitive pressures may sometimes dictate that such action and the attendant risks be taken. Generally, recruiting, training and assimilating new staff, especially in the context of a fast-growing, youthful company, take time, care and attention. There are books available on these subjects and if there is any doubt in the mind of a director about the suitability of an organisation, group or individual, to build the necessary competence as part of a new initiative, further reference, study, deep thought or action may be necessary. A section follows later in this chapter on training and staff development related to internationalisation.

DEFINING THE MARKET AND POSITIONING THE PRODUCT

It is important that senior management define the market, clarify the intent (for example, that a certain product for industrial marking is to be aimed initially at the electronic components marking sector exclusively) and communicate this information to all involved. Positioning the product is equally important and, to do it successfully, a knowledge of competition, customer requirements and the industry to be served is obviously essential. One particularly useful volume for reference on the whole subject of marketing strategy and company and product positioning is McKenna (1985). McKenna's 'four golden rules' of product positioning are as follows:

- Understanding the environment
- Focusing on the intangibles
- Finding the right targets
- Experimenting and changing (product positioning is not 'a one-time shot').

If those who are to market and sell a new product or sell any product into a new market have a clear idea of a strong sales platform which relates the value of the product to the customer and have adequate information to back up claims, they will fare much better, especially in a competitive environment. The 'intangibles' mentioned by McKenna are those which raise the discussion with the customer above the obvious issues of price and comparisons of difference in devices. In the technology business, where a new chip is invented every hour and equipment changes once a month, if customer decisions were only based upon device or price it would be extremely difficult for companies to sustain market positions and growth. A company like IBM or Hewlett Packard, to take examples from the computer field, does not offer devices *per se;* it clearly offers packages to enable customers to perform certain tasks, or sometimes a complete service from consultation to installation, training of people, and all necessary after-sales service and support. The customer investing a large amount of money in a significant computer system is likely to be persuaded by arguments which could be defined as relating to intangibles such as 'four-hour service response time', or 'access to the Hewlett Packard information bank on computer use' or 'membership of a user panel' as a perceived means of getting more from a large-scale investment than from working with a company not offering such benefits. It could be argued that a 'four-hour service response time' and features such as the 'training of one's staff' are not intangibles, but we are making a distinction between the product that is seen and runs on the bench and what the customer *really* purchases. When working through third parties such as overseas distributors, much time may be required to develop an appropriate understanding of product positioning in the minds of those who are to represent the company overseas. Another excellent and practical book dealing with this type of marketing approach in the fast-changing technology business is Davidow (1986).

'PRODUCT POSITIONING' – A DOMINO CASE STUDY

In Chapter 3 I referred to a particular decision in a particular company, Domino Printing Sciences plc, to move from a single technology into a second, but not essentially new technology, to serve applications different from (but not entirely unrelated to) those served by its core products. The technology new to Domino, which it acquired from a German company, was found to offer unusual if not unique features which enabled an ink-jet carton coder to print with water-based inks not only onto cardboard cartons but also, with the development of a new fast-drying solvent-based ink, onto less porous substances like plastic shrink film. All of this was taking place at a time when the packaging industry was moving quickly towards using more plastic shrink film and plastic-wrapped trays for cans rather than more costly complete cartons. Since established competitive products worked only with water-based inks, for reasons related to technology in selected fields of use, Domino demonstrated clear competitive advantage which also offered an opportunity to resist competitive price pressures. 'Positioning the product' for optimum awareness in the most appropriate places, however, took flair, energy and firm management in the home UK territory. The process of getting the product launched and successful in the UK took one-and-a-half to two years. All of this preamble is to highlight the important fact that, when working with trading partners in overseas markets to exploit this type of opportunity, much time, energy and attention to detail will be needed to ensure that the distributor:

• Understands the optimum market position and sales platform for the product
• Aims the product at appropriate customers in the correct market sectors

- Gets his advertising, PR and sales training right.

'Positioning' companies and products is a potentially rewarding but difficult process. It applies equally in the service industries; indeed, promoting and emphasising 'intangibles' and comparative customer benefits such as 'more understanding and responsive people to meet your needs' is often all a travel agent or a bank may offer even if the client invites it to say what its product can do and company X's cannot. In service sectors the quality of staff response to the client and clear professional standards are surely the real products. It is *doubly* difficult when working outside home territories and with third parties of various nationalities and culture.

What about the Domino case? How successful was the outcome? The usual story of great success in some parts of the world and a little less elsewhere!

INTERNATIONALISM AND 'WORLDTHINK'

As a company begins to exploit foreign markets for the first time, significant considerations concerning the aptitude and competence of staff for a world-wide business become important. Let us consider the example of a UK company which is five years old and has been operating only in its home market but now sees the opportunity and the need to expand rapidly internationally. Elsewhere in this book consideration is given to the kind of organisation which needs to be established to deal with international and export businesses. There is, however, much more to be considered by the directors and management of any company which has pretensions to be truly successful and to become accepted as a major force in overseas countries. The chairman and directors of a company intending to expand abroad will need to have balanced international attitudes, and would hopefully have among them extensive experience of doing business internationally. If not, thought will need to be given at the highest level to either introducing a suitable managerial resource or using outside consultants to help those directors concerned think through and understand in depth the issues involved in bringing about change to make the company truly international in outlook and attitude. Companies have, of course, succeeded without going to these lengths if they happened to have a unique product which was pulled by demand into various markets in the world, but with so many truly global companies operating in the 1990s, and with developments such as the single European market well under way, the likelihood is that all companies seeking to be successful internationally in the future will have to spend a very great deal of time creating the right environment and taking care to ensure that the whole organisation is properly trained and orientated.

Selection and Recruitment

Once a company is aware of the need or desire to enter overseas markets, it should be clear that staff selection and recruitment should be adjusted so as to build in characteristics in new employees, especially managers and those who will interface with overseas contacts, such as work experience in one or more overseas territories and language ability. Also during the selection process, the attitudes of individuals to travel and trends in international trade will need to be explored at length. In-depth knowledge of specific territories, of geography and international economics, will need to be added to the list of requirements of managers to be recruited.

'Worldthink' Environment

Domino is an industrial company of 600 people rapidly expanding in world markets. All of its central research and development and product planning are carried out in Cambridge, England. Even with its international outlook, there is a natural tendency for staff to focus on the local scene and local requirements. Most of them are British. In this environment, the chief executive and other directors have taken a strong position in constantly communicating the concept of 'worldthink' as a means whereby the company can maintain leadership and grow into the future by focusing on those markets around the world which are most prominent and offer the most in terms of future growth. 'Worldthink' conditioning can be exciting since a very great deal of information can be provided for staff about international affairs and, in particular, about the success of the company, its products and its people in various regions. In the early days of entering the international arena, of course, there may not be many success stories, but there can be situation reports from those visiting countries for the first time which can often give exciting insights into 'what might be'. The 'worldthink' message needs constant reinforcement.

Special Training, Coaching and Development

Geography and International Trade

In a company which is established but is attempting to enter international markets and to use existing staff either to visit overseas territories or to work at base in support of overseas business, training in geography and international economics and international trade should be undertaken. This can be done with the help of outside agencies or by knowledgeable management. The likelihood is that management in a growing company will be stretched and unable to undertake this entire burden. However, a mixed programme of activity involving specialist outside help and managers from within may be the ideal.

Languages

It should be obvious that when dealing with overseas countries language ability is very helpful. It seems that English is now the international language of business. This is good for those of us based in the United Kingdom and the USA. However, there are still parts of the world where ability with the local language is essential, and in most parts of the world it is a very considerable advantage, since it can enable much better and clearer communication than sometimes occurs when the overseas trading partner has people with limited English-language capability. In the case of Japan, companies in Europe and the USA have particular problems due to the unfamiliarity of the Japanese language, but in more and more instances one sees them tackling Japanese by either having local staff taught the language or employing Japanese staff in the organisation. It has been noticeable in the past two years that because of the increasing demand for language training in industry, the choices available to companies have increased dramatically, with many language schools and individuals offering highly flexible tutorial programmes. It is possible, in most parts of the UK, USA and major continental European countries, for companies to arrange for language tutors to visit company premises for group or individual sessions, or to visit the homes of employees. A further alternative is for the employee to attend the home of the tutor. Distance learning is also an area of significant development in language training, and indeed the language training area is an excellent example of the service industry growing fast to support changing patterns of industrial activity.

The Importance of Cultural Understanding

Have you ever met the sort of person who speaks nine languages perfectly and yet cannot communicate effectively in any of them? Good foreign business relationships cannot be built on the foundations of language ability alone. An appreciation of cultural differences is also of great importance. In addition, of course, a linguist is not a marketing manager just because he is a linguist – he needs to have been specifically trained in marketing. Hiring linguists to do international business could have catastrophic consequences if their language ability constitutes their entire training.

Training staff to attain an in-depth understanding of cultural differences, then, is in some ways more important than language training. Attendance at such courses as those run by the Centre for International Briefing at

Farnham Castle or those run for executives at business schools like INSEAD in Fontainebleau, France, together with coaching by experienced managers who can sit in on meetings with foreign partners and point out afterwards what really went on, can help create truly responsive and effective managers of foreign relationships. Relationships with foreign customers and trading partners will best be forged and maintained if relevant personnel have taken the time to understand not only how business is done by them but also how they relate to and behave towards each other. Understanding customer practices, culture, and how to participate in meaningful discussion and develop deep understanding, can make the difference between great success and abject failure in exploiting foreign markets.

IMPLANTING OR TRANSFERRING MARKET AND CULTURE KNOWLEDGE

The following three examples illustrate how the importing or exporting of culture, knowledge and skill have contributed to the successful exploitation of overseas markets by a UK-based industrial equipment company: (a) supporting the presence in its core UK marketing group for one year of a manager from the staff of a Japanese-based trading partner; (b) engaging the son of the owner of the company's Spanish trading partner and having him work at UK headquarters for more than a year; (c) placing a British financial controller on two-year secondment in the company's German subsidiary which was growing fast and was in need of skilled administrative support. The importance of understanding cultural issues and differences when seeking to exploit overseas markets has been emphasised. Language is also important. Even though the company in question had an array of European linguistic abilities spread over a range of staff, Japanese was not a local strength!

How did these 'exchange visits' help the UK company and thus justify the expense? In the case of the secondments from Spain and Japan the benefits included the following:

- Immediate improvement in communications between the company and its Spanish and Japanese partners, *especially* the latter.
- Improved understanding of operating problems, issues and needs in Spain and Japan.
- Fast resolution of problems leading to additional orders (*major* new growth in Japan).
- In-depth understanding developed by the Spanish and Japanese visiting managers of British culture and the UK company's culture, style and management processes. This insight into 'how to get things done and

who to go to for what' proved invaluable once the managers had returned to their home countries.

- Improved understanding in the host company's management group of Spanish and Japanese culture, the style of the Spanish and Japanese trading partners and particular problems/needs in those two countries. The ability to 'worldthink' in the host company management group was enhanced.

- An enhanced level of teamwork and rapport between the UK company and its Spanish and Japanese partners! *People* related better having been exposed in a work environment to *real Spanish and Japanese people!*

In the case of the financial controller posted to Germany, the knowledge transfer initially (and the case is still in progress) was largely:

- To bring the standards and requirements of the parent company and matters financial and administrative *immediately* into practice in a fast-growing German subsidiary.

- To improve data flow *immediately* from Germany to the group finance function.

- To educate a UK manager in depth about the culture, geography, industry, economics, and language of Germany; the specifics of 'our business' in Germany; and German management and accounting practices; as well as to give him experiences of working and learning overseas.

The knowledge and experience gained will continue to be put to excellent use when the individual returns to UK at the end of the secondment, by which time he will have established a finance function of excellence and appointed a German national as successor to himself in Germany. Many similar cases should be cited. For larger companies, these kinds of investment may not be uncommon or difficult to make. For small or medium-sized companies, the decisions may be tougher. But the risks and costs are definitely worthwhile.

There are less costly ways of bringing foreign country, industry and cultural knowledge to any home country. Half-year or one-year placements in UK companies of French and German industrial sandwich course students can be very beneficial. There are particular Anglo-French and Anglo-German three- or four-year business studies degree courses which give the opportunity to British companies to utilise French or German nationals of high calibre in positions which are primarily for training but which bring benefits similar to those described earlier in the Spanish and Japanese cases. Mature students can contribute both locally to improve cultural understanding and by contact with and support of overseas trading partners. Typically the sandwich course students would be engaged as marketing assistants. They may even become candidates for full-time employment in the UK or their home country upon graduation – a wonderful and inexpensive way to hire already partly-trained compatible people to help further exploration and exploitation of overseas markets.

MARKET PLANS, PRODUCTION AND LOGISTICS

The need for business planning has been covered in an earlier chapter of this book. For each market, be it overseas or otherwise, a simple plan needs to be developed early on as part of organising for new initiatives, and this plan must be distilled into numbers which can be translated into production volumes and which can also become the basis of inventory and distribution planning. Whatever the product involved, market plans, including all of the detailed differences which might be required by different overseas markets, must be expressed and regularly revised, and the interface between production and those responsible for marketing into new sectors and countries is a critical one. In the industrial field, where lead-times on parts for complicated equipment can be months, this is particularly important. The Domino Group runs a highly effective monthly operating plan review in the European and American operations where sales forecasts, production plans, sales history of each product, are scrutinised and debated by a multi-functional group, and out of this activity is distilled the means to fill orders quickly and meet business commitments. Meeting delivery dates is an important aspect of satisfying customers and succeeding with new initiatives. Planning is the only way to make it happen.

INTEGRATED PROMOTION ACTIVITIES

When organising for new market initiatives, whether these be in a market sector with one company responsible for all of the activities, or whether it be entering a new country or launching a new product in existing country markets, the need for properly integrated promotional activities covering exhibitions, advertising, sales literature, training and all of the aspects of the mix, will need a great deal of attention. When working with distributors, it is the principal producer and supplier who will need to take the initiatives and work with distributor management to ensure that the responsibility and cost of promotional activities are properly shared and also that wasteful overlap is avoided and, more particularly, that the messages about products and services are consistent.

For fastest and assuredly professional advertising, literature, product documentation and other materials, the safest, but not the cheapest, route is to generate material in all common languages within the structure of planned promotional campaigns *at source*. Trading partners *can* handle the printing and bulk production locally; some companies prefer the alternative of providing initial stocks from the home country in the language of the trading partner. When following this route, local proof-reading and approval will be necessary to avoid errors and gain the distributor's support. A centrally generated product advertising and positioning programme can be powerful, fast and broadcast a cohesive, clear message world-wide. Domino, for example, uses a similar advertisement translated into eleven different languages.

GETTING THE MONEY IN, CREDIT CONTROL, SALES AND ACCOUNTS

For a company which has previously only operated in the home country and is entering overseas markets, it is particularly important to think about getting the money in. Payment practices vary from country to country. The agreement struck with a distributor should clearly state the payment terms, and while these will need to be in line with custom and practice in the territory, they must also be negotiated in the best interests of the supplying company. Proper advice needs to be sought on protecting the supplying company's interests and reducing its exposure by organising for payment to be secured in specific ways. When working with less stable economies, instruments such as irrevocable letters of credit are, of course, essential. It is also recommended that companies take out suitable insurance against overseas credit problems and bad debts. A number of insurance companies offer such services, which may be known as Export Credit Guarantee Schemes, often approved by governments. On a more practical note, the interrelationship of the sales staff with accounts departments needs to be very close and at the start of a new initiative involving overseas marketing, joint briefings of the groups involved by senior management can be very helpful. Responsibility for debt collection needs to be clarified. Is it the salesman who is primarily responsible, or is there a credit controller from home base who is assigned the task? All of this needs working out in advance, as do decisions on which currency is to be used for billing. Some UK-based companies heavily involved in international business have billed entirely in sterling during periods in their history when all of their costs were in sterling. This tended to reduce the exposure of these companies, although it meant that they missed out on potential gains caused by currency movements. Decisions on how these things should be done are very much the province of the individual company, but it is extremely important that they be considered and the company is organised in advance for credit and treasury management.

PERFORMANCE INFORMATION, MEASUREMENT AND TRACKING

Once an initiative has been established, one assumes that management will wish to ensure that performance is tracked. If a company is exploring and exploiting overseas markets for the first time, the management information system may need to be developed in order that performance information compared to plan is provided to the right people. It has been said many times that 'You cannot control what you cannot measure'. It would be hard to argue against this principle, and so when setting up any new initiative responsibility must be assigned for ensuring that performance information comes in and is reviewed by the right groups.

QUALITY OF RESPONSE

Company-wide quality is the responsibility of every individual. The most common complaint from distributors, agents and customers – especially as concerns new products and new markets – is that the speed of response to identified requirements and to technical issues affecting customers, is below that which is expected. Company-wide attention to detail and constant training and retraining on quality and customer awareness are issues which again and again return to the forefront when we assess why some companies are consistently more successful than others with similar products or services. The accumulation of small things well done, incrementalism, attention to detail – there are no substitutes for these in ensuring proper organisation for the success of new market initiatives.

A final point about organising for new market initiatives. It is vital that the chief executive and directors take pains to visit all parts of an organisation about to launch a new initiative, and inform all staff, either directly or through briefing groups, of what is going on and how important the initiative is to the company. Only in this way will they generate the excitement that can go with thoughts of entirely new worlds to be explored, and ensure the understanding, motivation and dedicated support of their workforce.

CHAPTER 10

—— ❧ ——

AWARENESS AND ATTENTION-GETTING IN A NEW MARKET

We have already had something to say about the need for integrated approaches to promotion. This chapter discusses in a little more detail some of the ways in which in the early days of involvement a company may generate suitable levels of awareness of itself, its products and services.

ADVERTISING AND PROMOTION

A complete advertising and promotion campaign may be initiated from the headquarters base of a company entering a new industrial market in the home country and doing everything under its own steam, just as described in Chapter 9. An industrial company entering new markets in a second country through third-party trading partners will obviously have less control and is likely to share the costs. Advertising can be expensive and in the early stages of an involvement if the company is to get its own identity understood and is to share the limelight with a third-party trading partner, it will need to find a way to influence the messages and the quality with which they are conveyed and the media which are selected. It is often the case that UK exporting companies leave advertising and promotion entirely to the distributor, who will naturally emphasise his own identity. It has not been unknown for distributors to ditch suppliers and substitute one product for another. This is very easy for them to do if their own identity is the only one customers have been aware of. Therefore, when agreements are thrashed out, having a balanced understanding of the content of advertising material and the media used would enable a company making new initiatives to gain a degree of awareness from the outset.

EXHIBITIONS

For companies in the industrial, office- or consumer-equipment field, or in businesses such as furnishing and household goods, exhibitions are often a tremendously important way of gaining awareness for products, the company itself, its style and image. In particular, in an industry such as industrial equipment the trade show or exhibition is often the annual or biennial shop window for all or most of the significant purchasers in that field. When entering new regions or countries, exhibitions can be even more important and here again the supplying company will need to take an assertive position with a local trading partner in order to ensure that if his products are but one component of the distributor's portfolio, adequate coverage is given to his own business. It will often be agreed between the supplying company and the distributor that exhibitions are joint affairs and that the costs will therefore be shared. Making the investment and sharing the financial burden is an effective way of ensuring an appropriate amount of say in what is exhibited and how it is done, and this is strongly recommended. Industrial equipment companies and medical supply companies often plan exhibitions jointly with distributors and share the cost, also providing key technical and sales staff who support the distributor's own staff by their presence at the exhibition.

PUBLIC RELATIONS, DISTRIBUTOR AND CUSTOMER RELATIONS

Public companies in the UK tend to be involved in at least three kinds of public relations: corporate/city and investor relations; trade public relations relative to the product or field of use; and local community relations. When companies find themselves in partnership with distributors in different regions of the world they often find they are working with relatively small companies. Such companies may have little activity of their own in PR. The extension of home-based image-building, with suitable foreign-language translations which also take culture into account, can be extremely helpful to a company undertaking marketing initiatives overseas. Large industrial customers in overseas markets may very well be influenced to purchase from companies with a clear international identity as well as evidence of a strong financial position and a satisfactory quality record. An investment in public relations can help create the right impression and can assist a local distributor in a far-off land to present his own company and the principal in an excellent light and pre-empt the kind of knocking competition which is often encountered from local producers who may attempt to fill the minds of potential customers with doubts and negative thoughts about the principal. While public relations requires a professional hand at the helm, agencies tend largely to be co-ordinators of information and activity and the real public relations managers in any organisation are the chairman, chief executive and their teams.

CONFERENCES AND OTHER SPECIAL EVENTS

While dealing with public relations we can reflect on the usefulness as part of new market initiatives of special events either run by or sponsored by companies in support of the market or product introduction. Major health care companies often use the professional medical conference as a major activity in preparing a health-care environment for the introduction of a new therapy and the launch of new products. The impact of such events, drawing together leaders of a profession under the sponsorship of a commercial company and under the eyes of regulatory authorities, government and patients, can be a highly potent event. In the field of kidney care I have been involved in a dramatic example where a campaign including a conference together with numerous other activities, co-ordinated and sponsored by an ethical company and involving physicians, surgeons, interested parliamentarians and health-care and patient associations, not only brought about the successful world-wide introduction of a new treatment for kidney failure, but also changed the environment and government priorities in countries like the UK to a point where health-care budgets were adjusted and more money was made available for the treatment of patients and the purchase of medical equipment.

In a different example, the pharmaceutical industry itself has participated in a conference run by a producer of industrial marking equipment at which senior managers from the industry were brought up to date on the regulations for product identification in the pharmaceutical industry, were presented with information on the latest product development to meet the need, and were given three case studies by well-known executives from the industry itself to show how the specific product identification problems had been tackled.

This kind of conference, as part of a new marketing initiative, can indeed be powerful and in the industrial, medical and some consumer fields is always worth considering. In service industries the conference approach to gaining awareness can be equally effective. Consulting firms, for instance, frequently use the conference or seminar medium to make contact with potential customers in new geographical areas or if they are about to offer a new product. Merchant banks and financial service companies often seem to be running seminars on mergers and acquisitions (or how companies can avoid these!). The consulting arm of Investors in Industry (3i's) has been very successful in running lunchtime conferences and seminars to present new approaches to business planning, including the demonstration of software packages which can be acquired by clients together with the appropriate consulting expertise to put them into use in companies.

AGENCIES AND THIRD-PARTY HELP IN EXPLOITING NEW MARKETS

This subject has been touched upon in earlier chapters of this book. Public relations, advertising, the running of conferences, the gaining of awareness and attention do require focused and specialist resources. Much can be done by management itself, but in most circumstances, especially when starting to gain awareness in a new country, the use of a professional agency is likely to be essential. UK- and US-based companies working with overseas distributors may find that the trading partner has connections with a suitable firm. A number of international distributors have recently come to me and asked for help in co-ordinating and disseminating useful information about my company, Domino, because they felt the need for simple summaries of much of our marketing and financial information, and they genuinely believed there were opportunities for making much better use of material with professional help. They have also, in a number of instances, asked for specific help in approaching the press, organising press conferences and press lunches, and briefing the press pre-emptively. In some countries competitors had been known to present misleading information about the company, and its trading partners were anxious to have professional help, not in answering criticisms but in organising positive events ahead of time so as to make the competitors lose all credibility when spurious arguments were made after the customer had been properly informed. A corporate communications agency was commissioned to work on these international matters and the chief executive became involved in the preparation of programme material and in attendance at press conferences, together with the owners or managers of key distributors. This had the very positive effect of not only gaining local publicity but also creating an awareness of a combined activity, and clearly showed the synergy which existed between the company and its overseas trading partners. This is not the place to consider in detail the selection of agencies – Jennings and Churchill (1988) is well worth consulting on this subject.

THE CHAIRMAN OR CHIEF EXECUTIVE AS A PUBLICIST

The leader of a company seeking to exploit new markets and particularly to develop an international awareness, presence and reputation for his company, needs to accept the role of 'chief publicist' world-wide. Whether he is publicising his company to existing trading partners or to those he wishes to join the fold, whether he is selling his company to a particular industry association or whether he is acting as the spearhead of a new product introduction, in a range of countries across the world, the head of an organisation is in the best possible position to get the ear of those required; even if he is not a confident communicator, with appropriate help he will be able to find the means to get messages across more effectively than third parties or others in the organisation. The presence of the head of a company at a conference, an exhibition, a new product launch, a press conference, together with a trading partner, means a very great deal to that partner and to those others present. It seals the commitment of a company to an initiative and provides access for customers, press, and potential investors to a leading member of the board. Apart from all of the positive business results it can bring to a company, it can be great fun and it can bring a wealth of new knowledge, experience and friends to the chairman or chief executive involved.

CHAPTER 11

~

COMMUNICATIONS AND A SENSE OF URGENCY

FOCUS ON THE CUSTOMER AND POSITIVE ATTITUDES

In Chapter 1 we made the point that customers are the most important decision-makers in determining the success of any business. In any programme to exploit a new market, there will inevitably be a very large number of activities to be planned. Managers and others will be under pressure, relationships may become strained, and cohesion and teamwork may be difficult to sustain. As with all aspects of business, bringing people continuously back to a focus on the customer, the customer's requirements, the opportunities open to the company to satisfy customers, can be tremendously helpful in maintaining positive attitudes even when the hours being worked are long and nerves are frayed. Finding customers, winning them, satisfying them, and doing it for profit, are the end-points to which people in every function in business can relate. Directors and senior managers can play an enormously important part in steering the whole company or a specific group through a new market-entry programme by constantly keeping informed those who need to know about progress, milestones when they are passed, and the overcoming of obstacles. By incorporating the continuing theme of 'success through satisfying the customer', they can help maintain the necessary positive attitude and purpose.

FIRST CUSTOMER IMPRESSIONS ARE CRITICAL

For a company entering a new geographical or regional market or a new industry or consumer sector – indeed, in any circumstance where the name or the product of a company has previously been unknown – the first impressions gained by intermediate customers such as distributors and agents and end-users or consumers will be extremely important and in some instances will determine the success or failure of the venture. For the smaller company or the start-up company which might be introducing its first and only product, the introductory period can literally be a matter of life or death. In regions such as East Anglia in the UK, California in the USA, and in many developed countries, rapid technological advance has led to the formation of many start-up companies. The entrepreneurial spirit among inventive people with a good idea or a piece of engineering stimulates new companies to be set up. In recent years a large amount of venture capital has been available to encourage such start-ups. There have been a number of examples in the Cambridge area of England where start-up companies with excellent technology have spent two years developing a product and have journeyed through the period of preparation for market, have thought out good marketing plans and have produced excellent literature with a clear story and an apparently very sound sales platform for their product and have still not found commercial success due to failure at the first hurdle of real action – working with customers. Most of these companies are offering industrial equipment or domestic electronic equipment. In many instances the equipment requires the user to be well trained and adequate technical support to be available from the supplying company or its chosen distributors. Technical support is especially critical with a new electronic product of any kind since there are likely to be at least a few teething troubles. Start-up companies often fail to employ adequate resources to steer themselves through this first critical phase of product support, and at a time when they may well be using up the last of their venture capital and needing to expand sales rapidly, they can be seen in some instances to grow too rapidly, again relative to the provision of technical support. The result in some cases has been that a well-developed product which looked good in the literature and on the exhibition stand, gives the first customers who buy it a bad impression because of a lack of technical support, information or training. Since, particularly in industrial markets, customers buy products partly on common available information, bad words circulate and the company's name is immediately blackened. At the same time, for a start-up company, if the first few installations of a product requiring support necessitate the constant attendance of scarce technical and engineering resources at the customer site to get the equipment running, further sales and installations will be postponed or slowed down and a negative cycle of business can develop.

Because first customer impressions in new markets are critical, whatever the product, even when all aspects of introduction have been well attended and things appear to be going positively, there is a need to build into any new product programme adequate processes of feedback which can be done through sales groups, distributors, or through independent market research agencies. Very often in the early stages of marketing a product, customer response may give the clue to product enhancements that make an enormous difference to the competitive success of the new entry. British Airways has been referred to several times throughout this book. This is a large organisation which has changed its image and reputation: having once been perceived as a poor provider of service, it is now the world's most successful international airline and known to please most customers most of the time. Earlier in this book I referred to the research carried out by British Airways prior to the introduction of a new product for the first-class passenger. Immediately the product was introduced the interviewers were active in baggage halls with well-constructed questionnaires, gauging the early impressions of travellers not only about the product itself but particularly about the way staff were delivering the service during flights. Modifications to the product were immediately introduced, some of them very slight but all related to customer impressions and the need to satisfy customers for obvious reasons of competitive advantage.

New product launches and new market entries are often conducted in a highly charged atmosphere with a great deal of 'hoopla'. Exhibitions and trade shows can be exciting. Advertising can be attractive and stimulating. The period immediately following market entry or launch of any kind should be a period of tough-minded and challenging analysis review and questioning. The customers' first impressions should be a subject high on the list for discussion at such reviews.

OWNERSHIP AND LEADERSHIP

If the introduction by an industrial equipment company of a range of products into other countries is to be a complete success, the plans, discussed earlier in this book, which need to be made and implemented in detail, should define the specific responsibilities and roles of individuals. 'Ownership' of managers of the plan itself, and of the problems and challenges as they arise, will be essential. Often in business, and entering new markets is a good case in point, when things go wrong the fingers point in all directions. Company directors have an important role to play in setting the leadership example for all of those involved in a market launch. Making sure that everyone is aware of and excited by the plan is only the start. Encouraging managers throughout the organisation who are involved in the activity to take a leadership position in communicating successful aspects of the programme can be extremely valuable. Everyone can be a leader in one way or another as part of an exciting, if difficult, entry into a new market.

Once the action has begun, if the ownership and leadership attitudes are in place, feedback should occur simply through the responsibility of individuals involved and not because of chasing and harrowing by directors and the senior management team. It can be extremely helpful and positive for all concerned to publicise what some companies call 'little victories'. The first machine order is an important little victory when selling industrial equipment to a new market, and this can be publicised by the chairman or chief executive through memoranda and notices and pictorially highlighted in the company newspaper and the trade press. Encouraging an environment in which every little victory is reported, and taking an interest and ensuring availability of information at the level of the board, is not by any means an insignificant detail. It can be a major factor in generating the momentum required to crack a tough competitive overseas market.

INFORMATION TRANSFER AND POSITIVE WORLD-WIDE COMMUNICATIONS

Domino Printing Sciences plc is a medium-sized technology company which markets world-wide a range of products which have uses in every industry imaginable. New market sectors not previously perceived are being described with regularity. New uses of its products are being discovered by customers. Inventive applications for its products are being developed by its distributors, its subsidiaries, and in many instances its customers, who are combining the use of Domino equipment with computer technology, imaging technology and advanced engineering. In this kind of industrial business a sense of urgency in communication and the overwhelming desire to communicate exciting information about a new application can give a company a significant edge in that an exploitable market sector previously unheard of, a major new application which can win large numbers of new customers, can quickly become common knowledge around the world, if the spirit of co-operation and the will and the skill to communicate are present. Example 11.1 shows a simple medium used by Domino to communicate a newly discovered application world-wide. Example 11.2 shows a briefing note circulated together with an extract from a magazine article which indicated vast potential in a particular market sector for existing products.

Example 11.1 Information Transfer in Industrial Marketing.

Shown here is one of an ongoing series of technical/marketing publications used to transfer rapidly for world-wide exploitation information on *new applications* in specified industries of high technology product identification equipment. *Source*: Domino Group.

Domino Application Bulletin

SOAP SPONGES IN DENMARK

Customer:	Arbi-Skum A/S		Machine:	Solo 4/4
Location:	Denmark		Ink:	DA88
Application:	Coding sponges		Software:	Epson threeline
Substrate:	Foam		Linespeed:	25 metres/minute
Section:	Cosmetics/Toiletries/ Household			

Arbi-Skum A/S is a Danish company manufacturing and exporting various cleaning equipment for household purposes as well as industrial use, and specialised in soap-impregnated foam sponges.

For obvious reasons the customers of Arbi-Skum desired products marked with the logo of their individual company.

In this case, marking sponges, it was essential that the print did not disappear when the sponges became wet, nor be affected by general use. There was also a requirement for high quality print.

Furthermore, one customer in particular required a logo 25 mm high on the sponge.

To meet all these requirements, along with a quality print, Arbi-Skum was offered a Solo 4/4 printing with ink type DA88.

To allow printing of large logos, two standard printheads of the Solo 4/4 were positioned diagonally (staggered), as can be seen from the drawing overleaf. This enabled each printhead to code half the logo, a solution that turned out to be the right one.

To ensure the two prints matched precisely, the conveyor ran at a constant line speed.

Previously, this application was done by silk screen printing, with the result that ten out of a hundred sponges were incorrectly coded or simply not marked at all.

With the Solo 4/4 we have achieved an efficient and low-cost solution, fulfilling the demand for high quality print from Arbi-Skum and their customers.

Example 11.2

◆ Domino Sales and Marketing Bulletin

AWB/KLC

April 4, 1989

To: All Domino Subsidiary Managing Directors/President
All Domino Marketing Directors
All Domino Distributors
All Domino Salespeople Worldwide
All UK and US Graphics Personnel

MORE ON THE AGE OF IDENTIFICATION

OPPORTUNITY - as yet largely unrealised - WORLDWIDE OPPORTUNITY-that's what shouts at me from this interesting "Lithoweek" article I am circulating.

I was intrigued to see the prediction .... "most printers believe that ink jet systems will find their way onto Sitma lines in the UK by 1992".

Although we at Domino may have achieved a small number of exciting installations - and all credit to those who have done it - my main questions are about the future and what we need to do to get much more than our fair share of tomorrow's business - in those applications discussed in the article and more in graphics and commercial printing fields.

Domino Group management will discuss further steps which need to be taken to grow an ever stronger presence in these developing opportunity areas. Everyone copied - be stimulated by the proposals before us and look out for specific prospects. If you locate these and you are not working in Graphics for Domino - refer the information to Domino Graphics Group or distributor. If you are part of our Worldwide Graphics effort - you'll know what to do!

This should prove a useful piece for Graphics salespeople to generate stimulating discussions with potential clients.

Alan Barrell

Alan Barrell
Chairman

Enc.

Example 11.2 continued

But what of mailing systems of the future? Most printers believe that ink jet systems of the Domino and Videojet type will find their way onto Sitma lines in the UK by 1992. Ink jet technology will be particularly useful in this kind of application for two reasons: firstly because 50% of all jam-ups on the Sitma line currently occur on the label head, but secondly and more importantly because ink jets will make it much easier to achieve selective inserting. (*Lithoweek Supplement*, 15 February 1989, p. 23).

When a company is entering a number of new overseas markets, the communication of successful applications and the communication of successful methods of selling, demonstrating and satisfying customers, can be a tremendously important part of ongoing success.

What should not be forgotten is that the environment, the stimulus and the leadership required to ensure that all of this exciting communication takes place is the province of the chairman or chief executive. By taking an inspiring lead and setting an appropriate standard, he or she is in the best position to ensure a sense of urgency in all aspects of communications.

CHAPTER 12

---- ∾ ----

THE SINGLE EUROPEAN MARKET

The focus in this chapter will be upon the positive implications of the Single European Act (SEA), and European potential for companies operating out of the UK or the USA.

PRINCIPAL PROVISIONS OF THE SINGLE EUROPEAN ACT

The Department of Trade and Industry (DTI) offers a number of excellent publications for companies about the implications of the SEA. Excellent video presentations and advice for the director are also available from numerous DTI offices. *The Single Market – The Facts*, printed for HMSO in February 1989 (third edition) and available in the UK by dialling 01–200 1992, is an excellent preview and reference book which *all* directors should read. From this book I quote a summary of the main provisions of the SEA:

The [SEA] commits the EC to the aim of progressively establishing a single market over a period expiring on 31 December 1992. It defines the single market as 'an area without internal frontiers in which the free movement of goods, persons, services and capital is ensured in accordance with the provisions of this Treaty'. (The reference to the provisions of the Treaty is important to clarify the scope of the SEA commitment. For example, issues such as the control of traffic in illicit drugs and immigration from third countries are not covered by the EEC Treaty. Moreover, while Member States are working to reduce or abolish the barriers to the legitimate movement of goods and people, safeguards – like those on firearms, and plant and animal diseases – will continue for security, social and health reasons.)

The SEA also incorporates a series of important Treaty reforms to speed up decision-making by extending majority voting to virtually all the major areas of the single market programme. In the past, progress was often held up by the unanimous voting requirements which applied before the SEA came into force.

Progress towards completing the single market has taken as its starting point the Commission's White Paper, submitted to EC Heads of Government at the Milan European Council in June 1985. This outlined the Commission's programme for action to remove the remaining obstacles and distortions in trade between Member

States by the end of 1992. In welcoming the White Paper, the Milan European Council decided to draw up a precise programme of action based on the White Paper. Additional proposals are included in the programme as they are identified. [The DTI] Spearhead database [see p. 6 of *The Facts*] gives details of over 600 individual measures which are awaiting implementation, or are under discussion or are likely to be proposed by the Commission before the end of 1992.

Progress is already being made at an increasing pace. Some 275 individual measures have been approved since the 1992 commitment was agreed in 1985, including 125 listed in the Commission's June 1985 White Paper. That means around 45% of the single market programme in all, and the pace of agreements is continuing to increase now that majority voting applies for most single market measures.

Priorities identified by EC Heads of Government in June 1988 and reaffirmed at the Rhodes Summit in December 1988 include public purchasing, banks and other financial services, the establishment of common standards and intellectual property.

Also available from the DTI, and available in the same way, is *The Single Market – An Action Checklist for Business* (third edition, May 1989). Directors should obtain this and circulate it widely among managers. It stimulates thought and raises issues and questions about all aspects of business likely to be affected by the SEA and will help companies prepare for the great single market opportunity.

IMPLICATIONS FOR COMPANIES OPERATING ONLY IN THE UK

Some small companies will undoubtedly go on blindly operating in the UK or regionally within the country and will be largely unaffected by the advent of the single European market. Not all companies can be exporters and not all should attempt to be. However, directors of companies with no export ambitions or potential should explore the implications (which cannot be dealt with in detail in this book) relating to the potential for companies based in mainland Europe to penetrate more easily into the UK. They should carefully scrutinise the possibility that European companies in the period leading up to 1992 and thereafter could literally be 'after their business'. The implications of the single market after 1992 should be studied and understood and, in the case of small companies, some expert outside advice might be helpful. A strategy should be established as directors feel appropriate to protect the positions of the UK-only company.

THE SCOPE OF EUROPEANISM AND
GLOBALISATION

For those companies with expansive ideas, the desire to exploit opportunities wherever profit may be made would be a driving force were there no single-market legislation at all. Companies with products and services which have potential international appeal should anyway be planning and thinking globally.

The prospects of a market in Western Europe with a consumer population of 320 million, with a reduction in bureaucracy, with the destruction of trade barriers, with the free movement of goods and capital, should be an extremely exciting one. The development of clear plans for 'becoming European' are essential if these are not already in place. In my travels around the UK, I have heard a very great deal of discussion about 'protecting ourselves in readiness for 1992'. I have heard much discussion about 'the protection of British exports'. Some of this discussion troubles me and certainly disappoints me. It seems to me that the mentality of British exporters is likely to hinder them from taking full advantage of the true potential of a European market. Surely the companies which will succeed most in the single market of post-1992 Europe will be those companies able to take a truly European perspective, and yet able to convey in each individual country within the market sufficient understanding and knowledge of the local culture and business practice to be accepted as an integral part of the business community (this can happen either with a direct operation or through a local trading partner) rather than as an 'invader'. It seems that the European mentality is particularly difficult for us to establish properly in the UK. This problem clearly has historical roots and is related also to geography, since we are divided by a small stretch of sea from continental Europe. However, this will no longer practically be the case when the Channel Tunnel is open.

To all companies who seek to exploit the markets within Europe, I would say: 'find the means to become European'. The process of effective Europeanisation and profitable business growth in the markets of Europe will only happen if chairmen, chief executives and directors have the appropriate degree of understanding of what is going on, and are sensitive and sympathetic to geographical and cultural differences, and lead the whole of their own management group and company forward with a vision of greater potential and greater positive opportunity rather than taking a defensive and introverted stance.

EUROPEAN COMPETITION FROM 1992

European competition is already all around us. The reality of a single market is fast approaching and nothing will stop it. European as well as American and Japanese companies are already established in Britain. Domino already operates with excellent resources in all the EC countries and works incessantly to try and develop European understanding and European attitudes. Its European marketing group is based in Cambridge, England, and there is a constant need for staff to be supported, educated, steered and guided towards proper notions of European opportunity, which means, when planning a new product for European launch, going to the customers in all of the main countries to obtain your product planning information. Recently in the same company virtually all of the new product planning ideas were generated within the UK and the only structured market research and customer interview panel work was carried out in the UK. The company established an extraordinarily strong position in the UK, but not such a strong position in all European countries. Now, in discussion with staff, directors push the concepts of *European-think* and *Worldthink*.

Worldthink is an important concept because another aspect of the great European idea is, of course, that strong European companies may well be as large, through the inevitable industrial rationalisation which will take place, as the larger American and Japanese companies, and will be in a stronger position to compete globally once the single European market is realised. Therefore the wider our thinking, the broader our vision in taking advantage of the single European market, the larger the opportunities we may exploit with our companies or through creative collaboration with other similar companies. The implications are enormous and largely positive for all creative and energetic business people.

WHAT ACTION SHOULD COMPANIES TAKE IN CONTINENTAL EUROPE?

Much of the material and advice contained in this book is based on commonsense approaches to understanding and exploiting new markets. The principles constantly referred to are effectively the principles which should help a company towards success in the single European market. Many companies have established strong positions in Europe, not because when they set out with their plans they had the Single European Act in mind, but simply because they had the determination to explore and exploit all markets offering profitable business growth in Europe and indeed in the world at large. For some companies in businesses requiring substantial expenditure on product development with relatively short product life cycles, only by exploiting world markets and selling 70–80% per cent outside the UK can investments in new product development be returned. Thus, the principles of understanding the geography, the demography, the economy, the industrial base, the competition, consumer behaviour and other matters referred to in earlier chapters of this book, are the very things that must be understood and worked on for companies intending to assume leadership positions in exploring and exploiting the single European market. An added benefit to all of us should be that the single market will encourage a greater degree of standardisation of products, and will eventually bring harmonisation of regulations, performance and design standards etc. This process may take a long time but it is clearly written into the statutes which will determine the way in which Europe is run, if all goes well, in the future.

CHAPTER 13

―― ❧ ――

LAST PRINCIPLES

We set out on our journey at the beginning of this book with some thoughts on 'first principles'. Let us recall those opening statements:

- *Customers* are the most important decision-makers (not managers) in determining the success of a business.
- To satisfy customers consistently, the first thing a company needs is to have very clear aims and objectives. These must be shared collectively throughout the company.

We went on to discuss what a customer is, customer decision criteria and how companies can meet these. A company-wide approach to quality in all that is done and ways of clarifying aims and objectives were discussed at the beginning of this book. These first principles should become the working basis of our activities in exploring and exploiting new markets. But, having gone through processes of analysis of opportunity, prioritisation, decisions on action, the plans and the action 'live', how do we *measure* what we are achieving? Whatever our business, it is clear that the *results* of new market activities must be objectively assessed. How do we do this?

THE COMPANY ASSESSMENT

If we have been true to some of the principles discussed in the preceding pages we will have entered our new market with a business plan and with a properly constructed forward plan of profitability. We will then have the means to measure our performance against the plan. In addition to assessment of the results achieved in terms of sales, profits, market share and other factors, directors will want to understand how well a consumer or technology product has been received in a new market, and what the difficulties, the reservations, the competitive responses, have been. The company assessment of the success of an effort to exploit a new market is an ongoing process and should be the subject of regular review. Such review does need to be extremely well constructed and objective, and must relate to the original plans and measurable objectives.

THE CUSTOMER ASSESSMENT

The relative success of any launch of a company and/or its products into a new market must be looked at not only in terms of the internal data by which the company will measure its results, but also by the assessment of those primary decision-makers – customers. We examined in Chapter 11 some aspects of gaining rapid feedback from customers after the launch of a new initiative. Whether or not our early results have been good, there is a great deal of logic in structuring customer assessments of our activities and the performance of our staff and of the third-party distributors we may have employed. It is too easy to be lulled into a false sense of security by good early results. We must, if we are to be true to our belief that customers are the most important decision-makers in our business, place alongside our own data information from customers about their perceptions of all important aspects of our products and service. This can be done in industrial marketing by asking a sample or all of those customers taking delivery of our product for the first time to complete a questionnaire and meet a member of staff to discuss in depth objective assessments and feelings about the way products have been supplied, supported and the degree of success with which they have achieved the customer's objectives. In larger companies this analysis will be done by internal staff. In smaller organisations it is likely to be accomplished with the help of specialist market research agencies.

CUSTOMER SURVEYS AND USER PANELS

Customer surveys need not (and should not) be limited to the period immediately following the launch of a company and its products into a new market, or the launch of a new product. Different kinds of customer survey are very helpful if conducted on a regular basis either by staff in the company, or by independent agencies not connected with the day-to-day routine sales and service contact provided by the company to the customer. A regular flow of information from customer surveys and the results of user panel discussions can be of enormous help to new product planners, research and development departments, and not least to directors of companies. If the customer is the most important decision-maker in determining the future of any business, it seems appropriate to remain in touch in appropriate ways and for directors to assess the results of this ongoing communication process.

Domino Group organises a number of user panel meetings attended by selected staff members from the multinational companies it supplies. Those attending these meetings regard it as extremely important and are impressed if the chief executive or chairman appears for the entire meeting or for a particular session when views are being aired, or even finds the time to join such a group for lunch. When attending such meetings some of the information I have picked up has been very useful – the kind of information filtered out by management and thus would never have been acted upon. In the same way as taking value from user groups, chairmen, chief executives and directors will find enormous benefit in maintaining regular contact with real live customers using the products of the company. Field visits to customers employing products for innovative purposes, or to meet with the senior management of aggrieved or unhappy customers and in-depth discussions with those who are the first to use new products, are all enormously important and potentially useful activities for board members.

ASSESSING BUSINESS PERFORMANCE

This is not a technical book which sets out to provide information on the methodology available for assessing business performance. Each group of directors must decide, when taking a new market or new product initiative, on the criteria to be used in measuring the success of the initiative. This will inevitably relate to measurements of sales, profits, return on investment over defined periods of time. It will be necessary for a structure of information flow and review to be established in advance of the launch of the initiative, and for staff to be well informed of the requirements they will have to meet for the provision of information and also to make themselves available for the review activity.

In many companies new market initiatives are taken and either succeed, drift on, or end in failure or by default. When actions have been initiated to exploit a new market opportunity or launch a new product it is imperative that directors adopt a principle whereby the initiative is regularly reviewed in an objective manner. If the company is a public company it is particularly important for directors to accept their responsibilities for optimising the use of shareholders' funds. Therefore, a regular review process which looks at monthly and quarterly results versus plan and trends, forecasts, the level of expense involved, the views of those running the project on its likely continued success or turn around from early disappointment; all of this is something which requires a structured approach, a commitment of time and some degree of attention to detail.

If the programme of activity has been planned in advance in detail to provide 'gates' which are predefined, allowing operating management and directors the opportunity to take decisions on whether or not to proceed with the activity, the process of evaluation and decision-making can be simplified and can become much more objective. If those concerned with the enterprise at the sharp end are aware that every, say, eight weeks the chief executive or executive directors or nominees of the board are to review the programme against specific expectations established in advance for the review time, and if all managers are aware that a sequence of results giving a certain pattern or falling below certain expectations will result in a 'no-go' decision, there is likely to be appropriate positive tension in the management process compared to an unsatisfactory and lackadaisical state of affairs where reviews are either infrequent or inconsistent in structure, content and style.

CHAIRMAN AND BOARD AS ASSESSORS AND STRATEGIC DECISION-MAKERS

In a very small company the directors are likely to be those involved in driving the business forward and leading the new market initiatives. In medium-sized and larger companies this is not so much the case since directors are concerned with strategy and policy and operations management is at the front end getting the job done. However, for any initiative which is absorbing significant resources of the company, it is clear that the responsibility of the chairman, the chief executive and the board is to take those significant strategic decisions which are in the best interests of the company. So if directors are to fulfil their obligations fully they will need continuously to monitor the results of new market initiatives. They must be the assessors of strategic options. They must be the decision-makers on choices for the company, they must remain in close touch with the implementation of new initiatives which are absorbing shareholders' funds, and they must have the final say on whether a strategic approach can continue based upon an assessment of results that are being achieved.

APPENDIX

───────────── ❦ ─────────────

DISTRIBUTION AGREEMENT
FOR INDUSTRIAL APPLICATIONS

....................................../THE IDEAL COMPANY LIMITED

Issue date: ....

Joseph N. Blough
Company Secretary

Distribution Agreement
For Industrial Applications

Entered into as of the .... day of .... 1990 between:

PARTIES:

1.   IDEAL COMPANY LIMITED, an English Company
       with its registered office at Cambridge, England (here-
       inafter called 'ICL')

2.   .... a company with its
       registered office at ....
       ....
       (hereinafter called 'the Distributor')

121

Whereas:

A. ICL is a supplier of printing equipment and related
consumables

B. The Distributor is prepared to market and support
such items within the Territory (as defined below)

NOW IT IS HEREBY AGREED AS FOLLOWS:

1. DEFINITIONS

Products | The printing equipment (hardware, firmware
and software) together with any related spares
and accessories and related consumables as
are listed in the then current Ideal Industrial
Distributor Price List

Applications | The applications listed and the definitions
used in respect thereof In Exhibit A hereto

Territory | ....

Conditions of Sale | The current Conditions of Sale of ICL as
amended from time to time. The Conditions
current at the date of this Agreement are
set out in Exhibit B.

Ideal Group
Company | Ideal Holdings plc and any company 50%
or more of whose voting shares are owned
directly or indirectly by Ideal Holdings plc

Payment Terms | The payment terms as set out in Exhibit C
hereto

2. APPOINTMENT

2.1

ICL hereby appoints the Distributor as a distributor of the Products
in the Territory for Industrial Applications upon the terms and
conditions of this Agreement for an initial period of 24 months
from the date hereof and thereafter subject to six months written
notice by either party.

2.2

Unless approved by ICL, the Distributor shall have no right to distribute the Products for any other fields of use including but not limited to Specifically Excluded Applications. This Agreement supersedes all previous Distribution Agreements between ICL and the Distributor relating to distribution within the Territory for Industrial Applications.

3. SUB-DISTRIBUTORS

3.1

The Distributor is permitted to appoint sub-distributors and agents for the sale and service of the Products for Industrial Applications in the Territory during the term of this agreement on terms and conditions thought fit by the Distributor subject to clauses 3.2 and 3.3 hereinafter appearing and the prior written consent of ICL.

3.2

All orders and inquiries made by sub-distributors or agents in the Territory shall be dealt with directly by the Distributor and not ICL and ICL shall have no contractual or other relationship with such distributor or agent.

3.3

Sub-distributors and agents shall be bound by the provisions of this Agreement as to confidentiality set out in Clause 12.

4. OBLIGATIONS OF THE DISTRIBUTOR

The Distributor shall:

4.1

use its best endeavours to market and service the Products throughout the Territory;

4.2

not make or attempt to make sales of the Products outside the Territory directly or through a third party without first advising ICL of any inquiry received and permitting ICL to fulfil the same if ICL so elects;

4.3

not make or attempt to make sales for Specifically Excluded Applications and refer to ICL all their inquiries or orders for Specifically Excluded Applications;

4.4

notify ICL of the requirements which affect the Products in the

Territory and which stem from:
– local regulations
– safety codes;

4.5
be responsible for arranging export licences and documents, customs
formalities and settling all charges arising from foreign sales by the
Distributor or its sub-distributors and agents as appropriate;

4.6
maintain at all times reasonable stocks of the Products (machines,
spares and consumables) to cover a two month operating period and
shall fulfil orders for them and make repairs (including warranty
repairs) with reasonable promptness;

4.7
have sufficient competent, trained engineers to adequately support
the customer base and to train its own sub-distributors, agents and
customer staff in the use and, where appropriate, maintenance of
the Products;

4.8
be responsible for its own advertising and sales promotion including
preparing, printing and supplying technical literature (including
translations) based where appropriate on information and supplied
by ICL (subject to approval by ICL of the use of the Trade Marks
vested in Ideal Holdings plc under Clause 13 hereof);

4.9
be responsible for all the Product support required in connection
with the Products sold by the Distributor or its sub-distributors
or agents and shall provide at its own expense a warranty no less
favourable than the warranty offered by ICL on the Products to the
Distributor;

4.10
give proper consideration to the interests of ICL in all dealings
which the Distributor undertakes in relation to the Products;

4.11
not make any representations or give any warranties or other benefits
binding or purporting to bind ICL in favour of any other parties,
except as expressly stated in the Conditions of Sale;

4.12
promptly inform ICL of any facts or opinions concerning the features,
specifications, method of operations, manufacture or use of the
Products and any use which is relevant to the interests of ICL;

4.13

subject to the provisions of Clause 13, not alter or remove or tamper with the marks, trade marks, numbers or any other means of identification on any products coming into the possession or custody of the Distributor and in particular not interfere in any way in the affixing of any of the trade marks used in relation thereto, the Ideal logo (if affixed) or production serial numbers;

4.14

not act in any manner which will expose ICL to any liability nor pledge or purport to pledge ICL's credit;

4.15

act as principal and not agent for ICL in all the Distributor's dealings with third parties including its sub-distributors, agents and end-users (save and except by prior written arrangement with ICL) and take necessary steps to make clear the extent of the Distributor's authority to act on behalf of ICL;

4.16

defray all expenses of and incidental to the distributorship hereunder incurred by the Distributor;

4.17

in every July during the existence of this Agreement consult with ICL on the performance of the Agreement and produce a marketing plan for the next 12-month period commencing 1st November including forecasts for sales and orders by specific category of the products;

4.18

at the beginning of each month produce for ICL a forecast of the demand for the Products (by type) for the next six-month period, and fully specified orders with order numbers to cover such demand for the first two months of that period together with preferred shipment by month;

4.19

each year to provide for ICL one copy of its audited annual accounts within 30 days of completion of such accounts.

5. OBLIGATIONS OF ICL
ICL shall:

5.1

produce or supply to the Distributor Products meeting the requirements of local regulations and safety codes as may exist from time to time in the Territory within a reasonable time from being notified of such requirements by the Distributor;

5.2

not act in any manner which will expose the Distributor to any liability nor pledge nor purport to pledge the Distributor's credit;

5.3

defray all expenses of and incidental to the agency hereunder incurred by ICL;

5.4

promptly inform the Distributor of any facts or opinions concerning the marketing and application of the Products which are relevant to the interests of the Distributor;

5.5

provide from time to time such technical information as shall enable the Distributor to prepare all necessary handbooks and instructions for use and service of the Products;

5.6

provide technical assistance and training to the Distributor upon the request of the Distributor at the expense of the Distributor.

6. SUPPLY OF GOODS TO THE DISTRIBUTOR BY ICL

6.1

The goods sold to the Distributor by ICL shall comprise the Products and shall be on the basis of the terms and conditions set out herein and the Conditions of Sale. In the event of any conflict between the terms and conditions herein and the Conditions of Sale the terms and conditions herein shall take precedence.

6.2

On the assumption that the order contains the complete specifications for the Products ordered and that ICL accepts such order ICL will use its best endeavour to deliver standard items within 60 days of acceptance of order and to deliver all other products as soon as is reasonably practicable.

6.3

Shipment of machines is to be ex-ICL's premises at Cambridge, England, and other consumables ex-ICL's premises at Bootle, Merseyside, England. ICL will pack the Products suitably before shipment in accordance with its current procedures at the Distributor's cost.

6.4

All labour (and travel costs for such labour) supplied in the Territory by either the Distributor or ICL to meet the warranty terms of the Conditions of Sale shall be at the expense of the Distributor other than salary costs of ICL staff. In addition to the other costs, the salary costs of ICL staff working in the Territory on non-warranty matters for the Distributors shall be borne by the Distributor.

7. PRICING & PAYMENT TERMS

7.1

It is agreed that the pricing structure is as follows: ICL shall issue an ex-works price list to its Distributors (including the Distributor), at which Distributors can buy the Products from ICL. ICL may increase prices after 60 days notice to the Distributor. Such increase shall not apply to any firm orders received prior to the issue of this notice.

7.2

Should an order be cancelled within two months of the delivery date ICL reserves the right to make a cancellation charge, subject to negotiation and stage of completion and nature of order.

7.3

Payment terms shall be as set out in Exhibit C hereto.

8. PERFORMANCE

8.1

The continuation in force of this Agreement shall be subject to the achievement of a minimum annual invoiced revenue level to ICL from the Distributor in year ending 31st October 1988 and any year thereafter as may be agreed by the parties prior to commencement of the relevant years. In the event that the parties fail to agree the minimum annual invoiced revenue level shall be one hundred and thirty per cent (130%) of the actual invoiced revenue level in the previous year. For the avoidance of doubt the annual invoiced revenue level to be achieved in the year ending 31st October 1988 shall be £......... .

8.2

For the purpose of this clause annual invoiced revenue shall mean the total invoiced sums actually paid by the Distributor to ICL in any 12-month period (excluding Value Added Tax and/or other sales tax, insurance, freight and packaging).

8.3

In the event that the Distributor fails to achieve the annual invoiced revenue level set for year ending 31st October 1988 or any year thereafter ICL may terminate the Agreement by giving six months' prior written notice.

9. MANUFACTURING RIGHTS

9.1

Nothing in this Agreement shall confer on the Distributor any rights to manufacture or modify Products (including not to copy or alter any firmware or software) except as may be agreed from time to time in writing.

9.2

The Distributor shall not distribute or assist any other person to distribute nor manufacture nor assist any other person to manufacture goods of the same description or performing the same functions as the Products or competitive therewith.

10. SALE OF GOODS BY THE DISTRIBUTOR

10.1

The Distributor shall be entitled to sell the Products at such price as it shall think fit.

10.2

The Distributor shall be entitled (subject to any statutory or other requirements) to describe goods as it sees fit subject to the inclusion of the marks referred to in Clause 4.13 or other marks agreed pursuant to Clause 13.

10.3

It shall be the responsibility of the Distributor to ensure that all the Products supplied by it to end-users conform with any description applied to them by the Distributor and that the products are of merchantable quality and reasonably fit for the purposes for which they are supplied.

11. ORIGINAL EQUIPMENT MANUFACTURERS

Nothing in this Agreement shall prohibit ICL from selling products directly to original equipment manufacturers or similar organisations for inclusion in or use with their equipment or systems and subsequent importation or exportation into or from the Territory. No monetary allowance shall be made to the Distributor unless the Distributor is required and agrees to provide suitable after-sales service on the basis of ICL's OEM policy. All other direct user enquiries received by ICL will be forwarded to the Distributor.

12. CONFIDENTIALITY

12.1

ICL and the Distributor shall each use its best efforts to ensure that its directors, officers, employees, sub-distributors, agents, customers and suppliers and those of its parent companies, subsidiaries and affiliates keep secret all confidential proprietary information of the party supplying the information (the 'Provider') transmitted or made available to the other party, and shall not disclose the same to third parties (including companies, subsidiaries and affiliates of ICL or the Distributor, as the case may be) without the express written consent of the Provider and the same confidentiality undertaking from the third party receiving the information.

12.2

Such confidentiality undertaking as in Clause 12.1 above shall not apply to information that has already been published or has been in the receiving party's possession other than through the Provider or a person deriving such information, directly or indirectly, from the Provider.

12.3

In the event that this Agreement is terminated, all such confidential proprietary information that has not by then entered the public domain shall be returned immediately by the respective parties to the Provider of such confidential proprietary information.

12.4

Except in furtherance of the distributorship hereby created neither the receiving party hereto nor any third party specified in Clause 12.1 shall use or utilise, directly or indirectly, confidential proprietary information of the Provider without the express written consent of the Provider.

12.5

The obligations imposed by this Clause shall survive the termination of this Agreement.

13. TRADE MARKS

13.1

The Distributor shall sell the Products under the trade names and trade marks the benefit whereof is vested in certain Ideal Holdings Companies. The Products for use in equipment for distribution by the Distributor in the Territory shall be marked 'Ideal'. The use of such trade names and trade marks in the marking, packaging and advertising of the Products in any event shall be subject to approval by ICL.

13.2

The Distributor shall obtain no rights to such trade marks or trade names and any use of such trade names and trade marks by the

Distributor shall be considered use by ICL. The Distributor shall
cease using such trade names and trade marks on termination of this
Agreement and the Distributor shall take all steps as are practicable
to ensure that the property in such trade marks and trade names
shall remain vested in the appropriate Ideal Holdings company.

13.3
The Distributor shall advise ICL of any infringement in the Territory
of such trade names and trade marks coming to the notice of the
Distributor.

14. PATENT LIABILITY

14.1
ICL gives the Distributor no indemnities and makes no warranties
whatever that the patent rights of third parties may or may not be
involved by the marketing or other exploitation of the products.

14.2
ICL and the Distributor accept that any liability for infringement
of third party's patents does not constitute a breach of ICL's or the
Distributor's obligations hereunder.

15. DURATION AND TERMINATION

15.1
This agreement shall commence on the date hereof and shall continue
until determined in accordance with this Clause or Clauses 2 or 8
hereof.

15.2
Either party may terminate this Agreement effective immediately
upon given written notice to the other party hereto in any of the
following events:

    (a)   a judicial finding that the other is insolvent or
           bankrupt;

    (b)   the filing of a petition for the bankruptcy or
           insolvency by the other or the filing of any such
           petition against the other or an application by or
           in respect of the other to any tribunal for a receiver
           trustee or similar officer to be appointed by any court
           or executive department to liquidate or conserve that
           other or any substantial part of its property or assets
           due to insolvency or the threat thereof;

    (c)   the other suffers any trusteeship or receivership
           to continue undischarged for a period of sixty

days or suffers any similar procedure for the relief of distressed debtors entered into by that other voluntarily or involuntarily or that other is divested of its assets for a period of sixty days

(d) an assignment by the other for the benefit of creditors;

(e) direct or indirect acquisition of 30% or more of the voting shares of the other party by a person or enterprise if such person or enterprise engages directly or indirectly in the manufacture, sale or distribution of any product which directly or indirectly competes with the Products.

If any party hereto should suffer in respect of itself any event of the type enumerated in a) to e) above, such party shall immediately notify the other party hereto of such occurrence of such events.

16. MODIFICATIONS

Any modification or alteration of the terms of this Agreement shall be in writing and signed by or on behalf of the parties hereto.

17. WAIVER

The waiver by either party of any breach of this Agreement shall not affect the rights of such party to subsequently enforce its rights.

18. CHOICE OF LAW

The validity, construction and performance of this Agreement shall be governed by and interpreted in accordance with the laws of England.

19. EQUITABLE REMEDIES

The parties hereto intend that equitable remedies, including specific enforcement, will be available against any party in breach of this Agreement.

20. NOTICES

20.1

Any notice or other communication required or permitted pursuant to this Agreement between the parties may be made by hand or air courier, fastest-rate cable or telex, or by telecopy, notice by cable, telex or telecopy to be confirmed by registered mail (registered airmail if across national boundaries). Notice made in accordance with the preceding sentence shall be effective on dispatch.

20.2

Notice shall be deemed sufficient if sent in the foregoing manner to the following persons;

If to ICL: Ideal Company Limited
                      Bar Hill,
                      Cambridge,
                      England
                      Att: Company Secretary
                      Telex:
                      Telefax:

If to the Distributor:

                      Att:
                      Telex:
                      Telefax:

20.3

The addresses, telexes and telefax numbers indicated above may be changed at any time by notice of such change.

21. FORCE MAJEURE

Anything to the contrary in this Agreement notwithstanding, none of the parties hereto shall be liable to any other party hereto for any loss, injury, delay, damages or other casualty suffered or incurred by such other party hereto due to strikes, riots, storms, fires, explosions, acts of God, war, governmental action, or any such cause similar thereto which is beyond the reasonable control of such first party hereto, and any failure or delay by any of the parties hereto in performance of any of its obligations under this Agreement due to one or more of the foregoing causes shall not be considered as a breach of this Agreement PROVIDED that each order shall constitute a set Contract of Sale and no one default in a shipment shall be a cause for terminating the relationship between the parties hereunder.

EXHIBIT A

Fields of Use

A. Industrial Applications:

Industrial applications include, but are not limited to, marking and coding in the following industries:
- Packaging:
    Includes but is not limited to pouches, cans, tins, boxes, crates, tubes, bags, sachets, sacks, aerosols, drums, phials, film, and bottles; and labels therefor.
- Industrial Products:
    Includes but is not limited to fabrications, components, tools and raw materials.
- Consumer Products
- Food Products (direct printing)
- Defence Product

B. Specifically Excluded Applications:

1. Computer Output Printers
2. Office Copiers and Duplicators
3. Calculators
4. Chart Recorders
5. Textiles and Wall Coverings
6. Cartographic Printers
7. Colour Plotters and Colour Hard Copy Devices
8. Document Facsimile and Electronic Mail
9. Oscillographic Recorders

10. Addressing and Franking
11. Application to printing plants and associated equipment
12. General off-line label and bar code printing
13. Commercial and Graphic Arts
14. Newspapers, Magazines and Books
15. Business forms, computer letters, documents
16. Banknotes
17. Security and fund transfer documents
18. Tickets, coupons and vouchers
19. Overprinting of numbers and text on sequential and non-sequential basis

EXHIBIT B

CONDITIONS OF SALE OF IDEAL COMPANY LIMITED
('the Company')

All quotations are made and all orders subject to the following conditions of sale unless expressly varied by the Company in writing. This Contract will be governed by English Law. Any concession, latitude or waiver that may be or may have been allowed by the Company at any time, shall not prevent the Company subsequently exercising their full rights under this Contract.

1. Contract
No contract is made with the Company until there has been an acceptance in writing by the Company of an order placed by the Purchaser. The Purchaser's order shall constitute an offer in writing upon the terms of the quotation by the Company which shall set out the specific goods and services for which a quotation is made and the terms and conditions on which they are available to the Purchaser.

2. Prices
Orders are accepted on the understanding that prices quoted are firm for a period of one month only from date of quotation. Prices quoted do not include VAT, delivery, packing, insurance and other similar charges unless specifically stated.

3. Delivery
Times and dates for delivery or performance are business estimates only and not contractual obligations of the Company. Time therefore will not be of the essence of the Contract and provided the Company makes delivery within a reasonable time (taking into account all the circumstances) the Purchaser will be bound to accept a delivery if made after the date fixed and shall not be entitled to repudiate the Contract or claim damages in respect of late delivery, unless the Company has specifically agreed in writing to the contrary on a contract by contract basis.

4. Terms of Payment
(1) In respect of any system orders (unless otherwise provided on the face of these conditions) payments shall be made as follows:
    (a) A part payment of 30% on acceptance of order
    (b) A part payment of 60% on delivery
    (c) The balance within 30 days of delivery
(2) Payment for other goods and services (including separate delivery, packing, insurance and similar charges) shall be nett 30 days after despatch.

5. Interest
Any payment not made on the due date shall thereafter carry compound interest at the rate of 2% per month accruing on a day to day basis until final settlement.

6. Cancellation
Should an order be cancelled within two months of the due delivery date the Company reserves the right to make a cancellation charge.

7. Inspection and Tests

The Company's products are carefully inspected and, when practicable, submitted to standard tests at the Company's works before despatch. If tests other than the Company's standard tests in the presence of the Purchaser or his representative are required, these will be charged. In the event of any delay on the Purchaser's part in attending such tests or inspecting the goods in order to accept the same, after seven days' notice that they are ready, the tests will proceed in the Purchaser's absence and shall be deemed to have been made in the Purchaser's presence and, notwithstanding failure to inspect the goods the Purchaser will be deemed to have accepted them.

8. Rights to Withhold Delivery

If the Purchaser should fail to make due payment of all monies due by the Purchaser to the Company on whatever account, until all such monies have been paid the Company is entitled to withhold delivery of the goods or any part thereof.

9. Storage

If the Company does not receive forwarding instructions sufficient to enable it to despatch the goods within 14 days after the date of notification that they are ready for despatch, the Purchaser shall take delivery or arrange for storage. If the Purchaser does not take delivery or arrange for storage, the Company shall be entitled to arrange storage either at its own works or elsewhere on the Purchaser's behalf and all charges for storage, for insurance or for demurrage shall be payable by the Purchaser.

10. Property in Goods and Purchaser's Risk

All goods are consigned at the Purchaser's risk but the property in the goods will not pass to the Purchaser until payment has been made to the Company of the full contract price of the goods. In the case of default by the Purchaser, the Company may give notice to the Purchaser terminating the Purchaser's right to possession whereupon the Company may (whether with or without previous notice) itself take repossession of the goods and the Company is in such circumstances irrevocably authorised by the Purchaser to enter the premises and to remove the goods. If not withstanding that the property in the goods has not passed to the Purchaser the Purchaser shall deal with the goods in such manner as to pass to a third party a valid title to the goods the Purchaser shall hold the proceeds of such sale on trust for the Company. The responsibility for any loss or injury after the date of consignment prior to the property in the goods passing to the Purchaser is accepted by the Purchaser as Bailee.

11. Claims in Respect of Delivery

Both carrier and the Company must be advised (otherwise than upon a carrier's documents) within seven days of expected time of arrival if goods are not delivered, or within seven days of delivery if damage, pilfering or shortage is revealed upon receipt of the goods. Provided that such notice is given the Company will endeavour to assist the Purchaser to obtain proof of delivery or admission of damage, pilferage or short delivery from carriers.

12. Complaints and Warranty

All usual and reasonable precautions are taken by the Company to ensure excellence of workmanship and material but warranties or conditions implied by statute or otherwise are hereby expressly excluded. Particularly the Company cannot accept responsibility for consequential loss or damage affecting persons or things attributed to the failure of the goods due to accidents abuse or any other reason whatsoever. Any goods supplied hereunder which are within 12 months of delivery found to be defective in materials or workmanship will be replaced or repaired by the Company provided that the Goods have not been damaged or have not been improperly installed or operated or for any other reason such defect is not properly attributable to any act or omission on the part of the Company and provided that the defective parts are promptly returned by the Purchaser free to the Company's works as soon as the defect or apparent defect is known unless otherwise arranged. Such repair or replacement shall be carried out at the expense of the Company. The Company shall not be liable for any delivery, packing or insurance charges. In any event the Company is to be liable for nothing more than the contract price of the goods the subject of the complaint. The use of inks or making of modifications which have not been approved by the Company shall invalidate any warranties.

13. Agents

The Company does not authorise any distributor, agent, dealer, or representative to make any guarantee or warranty on its behalf.

14. Force Majeure

The Company shall not be under any liability of whatsoever kind for non-performance in whole or in part of its obligations under the contract due to causes beyond the control either of the Company or of the Company's suppliers including, but not limited to, acts of God, acts of the Customer, or of a third party, war, sabotage, insurrection, government regulations, embargoes, strikes, labour disputes, illness, flood, fire, tempest, delay in delivery, to the Company or the Company's suppliers or shortage of any goods or materials. In any such events, the Company may, without liability cancel or vary the terms of the contract including but not limited to, extending the time for performing the contract for a period of at least equal to the time lost by reason of such event.

15. Patents

The Company gives no indemnities nor makes any warranties whatever that the patent rights or other industrial property rights of third parties may or may not be involved by the marketing or other exploitation of goods supplied by the Company.

16. Arbitration

If at any time any question, dispute or difference whatsoever shall arise between the Purchaser and the Company upon, in relation to, or in connection with the contract, either party may give to the other notice in writing of the existence of such question, dispute, or difference, and the same shall be referred to the arbitration of person to be mutually agreed upon, or failing agreement within 14 days of receipt of such notice, of some person appointed in accordance with the provisions of the Arbitration Act 1950 or any statutory modification or re-enactment therefor the time being in force.

17. Date

These terms and conditions are to be referred to as dated January 1984 and supersede any other previous terms and conditions in issue.

EXHIBIT C

Terms of Payment

1. For initial distributors (and established distributors failing to meet terms of payment under Paragraph 2) below, the terms of payment shall be as follows:

    1.1 In respect of any system orders:

      a) a part payment of 30% on acceptance of order;
      b) the balance of 70% within 30 days of shipment payable by international irrevocable Letter of Credit, in pounds sterling, confirmed by a first class London Bank, received in Bar Hill at least 7 days prior to shipment.

    1.2 Payment for other goods and services shall be nett 30 days after despatch.

    1.3 The terms of payment under this paragraph with the particular Distributor shall be subject to review by ICL after one year from the date of commencement of this Agreement.

2. For established distributors the terms of payment shall be, in respect of any system orders, a period of 40 days subject to agreement with the particular distributor.

3. ICL reserves the right to change the particular distributor from the terms of payment under Paragraph 2 above to the terms under Paragraph 1 above in any situation where in the previous six months 3 or more orders have failed to be paid by the due date.

4. Payment shall be made in pounds sterling.

BIBLIOGRAPHY AND FURTHER READING

Abegshan, James C., and George Stalk, jun. (1988) *Kaisha – The Japanese Corporation.* Charles E. Tithe Co.

Attwood, Peter R. (1971) *Planning a Distribution System.* Gower.

Battersby, Albert (1968) *Sales Forecasting.* Cassell.

Crosby, Philip B. (1978) *Quality is Free.* Mentor, New American Library.

Davidow, William (1986) *Marketing High Technology.* Free Press.

Foster, Richard (1986) *Innovation – The Attacker's Advantage.* Pan.

Goldratt, Eliyahu M., and Jeff Cox (1986) *The Goal.* North River Press Inc.

Goldsmith, Walter, and David Clutterbuck (1984) *The Winning Streak.* Weidenfeld and Nicolson.

Hardy, Leonard (1962) *Marketing for Profit.* Longman.

Harvey Jones, John (1988) *Making It Happen.* William Collins.

Jennings, Marie, and David Churchill (1988) *Getting Your Message Across.* Director Books.

Krausher, Peter (1969) *New Products for Diversification.* Business Books.

McKenna, Regis (1985) *The Regis Touch–Million-dollar Advice from America's Top Marketing Consultant.* Addison-Wesley.

Porter, Michael (1985) *Competitive Advantage – Creating and Sustaining Superior Performance.* Free Press.

Roth, Robert (1982) *International Marketing Communications.* Grain Books.

Sewell, J. L. (1966) *Marketing and Market Assessment.* Routledge & Kegan Paul.

Stacey, N. A., and A. Wilson (Third edn; 1963) *Industrial Marketing Research.* Hutchinson.

Stapleton, John (1982) *How to Write a Marketing Plan.* Golden Press. Auckland.

The World in Figures (annual). Economist Publications.

'Problem Solving Techniques'. Internal document. Domino Printing Sciences plc.

INDEX